Freedom of Expression Debates in Europe and the Muslim World after 9/11

LEXINGTON STUDIES IN CLASSICAL AND MODERN ISLAMIC THOUGHT

Hussam S. Timani

This series will explore and examine a vast literature on understudied strands in Islamic thought. The series topics include, but not limited to, Qur'an and hadith studies, classical theological and philosophical doctrines, the human knowledge, law and tradition, law and legal reforms, tradition and renewal, Salafi thought, piety movements, neo-traditionalism, neo-liberalism, neo-reformism, neo-Islamism, cultural pluralism, and liberal and ethical humanism. Additional subjects for consideration would be trends in contemporary Islamic thought such as democracy, justice, secularism, globalization, international relations, Islam and the West, and feminism. The volumes in the series would examine, historicize, and analyse Muslim intellectual responses to the various trends of Islamic thought that have been understudied in Western scholarship. This series would make an important and timely literature available to the English reader.

Titles in the Series

Freedom of Expression Debates in Europe and the Muslim World after 9/11, by Haris bin Aziz

God in Islamic Theology: The Theology of Tahwid in Said Nursi's Risale-I Nur and Classical Islamic Theology, by Mehmet Ozalp

On Pain and Suffering: A Qur'anic Perspective, by Abla Hasan

Forging Ideal Muslim Subjects: Discursive Practices, Subject Formation & Muslim Ethics, by Faraz Masood Sheikh

Decoding the Egalitarianism of the Qur'an: Retrieving Lost Voices on Gender, by Abla Hasan

Freedom of Expression Debates in Europe and the Muslim World after 9/11

Haris bin Aziz

LEXINGTON BOOKS
Lanham • Boulder • New York • London

Published by Lexington Books
An imprint of The Rowman & Littlefield Publishing Group, Inc.
4501 Forbes Boulevard, Suite 200, Lanham, Maryland 20706
www.rowman.com

86-90 Paul Street, London EC2A 4NE

British Library Cataloguing in Publication Information Available

Library of Congress Cataloging-in-Publication Data

ISBN 978-1-66693-470-0 (cloth)
ISBN 978-1-66693-471-7 (ebook)

This study is dedicated to my parents
Aziz Ahmed Qureshi and Zeenat Aziz
and most humbly presented to my spiritual mentor
Khwaja Shamsuddin Al-Azeemi

اگر سیاه دِلم، داغِ لالہ زارِ تو ام
وگر کشاده جبینم، گلِ بہارِ تو ام

Contents

Figures

Tables

Acknowledgments

First and foremost, I thank Allah the almighty for empowering me to complete this challenging study. Thanks are also due to my parents, my wife, Sana Asif, family, and friends for all their encouragement, support, and good faith in me regarding this undertaking. I am also greatly thankful to Dr. Uzma Shujaat, my principal PhD supervisor at the University of Karachi. She remained an inspiration throughout with extraordinary guidance, motivation, and support. I cannot forget to mention the University of Karachi because where I am today is because of my alma mater. I hope to be able to pay back a little of what my university has given me. I am also grateful to Dr. Michel Boivin and Dr. Claudio Cressati, my external PhD examiners who gave approval without any correction. I owe a lot of thanks to my elder brother Arshad bin Aziz and his family as phases of this study in UK were not possible without their extraordinary help, love and support.

Special thanks to Professor Richard Sorabji who went through my manuscript and encouraged me to move forward with his appreciating comments. I also thank Dr. Eugenio F. Biagini, my supervisor during my stay at the University of Cambridge and Professor Nicholas Lemann, my supervisor during my stay at Columbia University. Both professors accepted my proposal, held meetings with me, and guided me with valuable suggestions during the hard times of COVID-19. Dr. Russell D. Foster, my supervisor during my stay at King's College London was an inspiration and extraordinary help. Dr. Sergio Belardinelli, my supervisor during my stay at the University of Bologna, gave valuable suggestions that helped me greatly. Dr. Anu Masso, my supervisor during my stay as DoRa Plus Scholar at the Tallinn University of Technology, also helped me greatly to complete this research.

Dr. Joseph Downing, Fellow in International Migration at London School of Economics, also provided me with a clear direction. Dr. Khaled Fahmy kindly gave up his time at the University of Cambridge to meet with me and provide precious tips to move forward. Dr. Basil Mustafa invited me to the Oxford Centre for Islamic Studies, gave suggestions, and introduced me to Dr. Mohammad Talib and Dr. Moin Ahmad Nizami, which led to fruitful discussion. Dr. Thomas Hanitzsch, chair of the communications department at LMU Munich, kindly met with me to discuss this research project and provided helpful suggestions. Dr. Michael Haus from the University of Heidelberg, Dr. Christian F. Rostbøll from the University of Copenhagen, and several other academicians from premier institutions in Europe and the United States helped me with their suggestions and encouragement through emails. I also thank my friend Asad Ahmed for his encouragement, Dr. Shaista Tabassum, Dr. Muhammad Reza Kazimi, Munazza N. Kazmi, Dr. Tasneem Sultana, Musharfa Butt, and Ms. Sahar for their support. Here, I cannot forget Dr. Masuma Hasan from whom I learned the basics of academic research.

I express my gratitude to the reviewer of this manuscript for having approved it without any major amendments and for giving highly positive and encouraging remarks. The staff at Lexington Books—Hussam S. Timani, Trevor F. Crowell, Emilia Rivera, Joseph Parry, and especially Anna Debiec and Kayla Wittman—helped me a lot; a bunch of thanks!

I also thank my teachers the late Sheikh Mutahir Ahmed, Farhan H. Siddiqi, and Naeem Ahmed:

سر اٹھاتا ہوں اِسی خاک کی دشواری پر
اب مجھے دیکھ، میں آیا ہوں نموداری پر

Abbreviations

ACHPR:	African Charter on Human and Peoples' Rights
ACHR:	American Convention on Human Rights
AfD:	Alternative for Germany (party)
CFREU:	Charter of Fundamental Rights of the European Union
CEU:	Council of the European Union
DRMC:	Declaration of the Rights of the Man and of the Citizen
ECHR:	European Convention on Human Rights
ECtHR:	European Court of Human Rights
EDL:	English Defense League
ENAR:	European Network against Racism
FPÖ:	Freedom Party of Austria
HRW:	Human Rights Watch
ICCPR:	International Covenant on Civil and Political Rights
ICERD:	International Convention on the Elimination of Racial Discrimination
ICESCR:	International Covenant on Economic, Social and Cultural Rights
ICHR:	International Covenants on Human Rights
ISIS/ISIL:	Islamic State of Iraq and Syria/Islamic State of Iraq and the Levant
NDL:	Norwegian Defense League
OECD:	Organisation for Economic Cooperation and Development
OIC:	Organisation of Islamic Cooperation (Organisation of the Islamic Conference till 2011)
OSCE:	Organization for Security and Cooperation in Europe
ÖVP:	People's Party (Austria)
PEGIDA:	Patriotic Europeans against the Islamisation of the Occident
PVV:	Party for Freedom (the Netherlands)
SAP:	Social Democratic Party (Sweden)
SD:	Sweden Democrats (party)
UDHR:	Universal Declaration of Human Rights

UNESCO:	United Nations Educational, Scientific and Cultural Organization
UNGA:	United Nations General Assembly
UNHRC:	United Nations Human Rights Council
UNSC:	United Nations Security Council
USCIRF:	United States Commission on International Religious Freedom
USSR:	Union of Soviet Socialist Republics
V:	Left Party (Sweden)
VVD:	People's Party for Freedom and Democracy (the Netherlands)

Introduction

Freedom of expression emerged as one of the major debates between the West, particularly Europe and the Muslim world after the 9/11 attacks. Certain major controversial incidents led to the need to examine views of both Islamic and Western worlds to determine how they perceive the notion of the freedom of expression. There also emerged need to consider the circumstances that prevailed after 9/11 and that which affected Islam-West relations. The consequential impact of particular incidents on the Western, and particularly European, masses and media has also been a point to be given due importance.

In order to reach the core of controversy, it is imperative to understand viewpoints of scholars from both sides along with historical and chronological accounts of different pertinent events. It is also important to academically inquire about the reasons behind Muslim reaction against the concept of freedom in the West and Western viewpoint in terms of freedom of expression that proved to be the primary force behind propagation of certain publications, depictions, and/or broadcasts. Statements by the heads of states and governments, religious and political leaders, and heads of international governmental and nongovernmental organizations also exacerbated the debate in general and on particular incidents.

While examining the means of Muslim protest, it is pertinent to know what Islam says about human dignity and freedom, freedom of expression and religion as well as what are Islamic injunctions about blasphemy and apostasy. It is also significant to examine why Islam proclaims that it is a complete way of life and why it is so important for Muslims to give space to their religion in every walk of life. Post-9/11 events also highlighted the need to intrigue about prevailing anti-Muslim sentiments in the West, the impact of which was clearly seen on Western media after 9/11.

There are ongoing intellectual and legal debates in the West, particularly in Europe on religious sensitivity, laws governing freedom of expression, and religion in Europe along with pertinent court decisions. But less light has been shed on constitutional provisions in the Muslim countries on freedom of expression and religion and especially much-debated blasphemy laws and penal laws governing blasphemy.

In light of the preceding prefatory points, there is a need to understand version of Western world in terms of freedom of expression and to find out the reasons behind Muslim reaction at length as well. For this, a detailed study is necessary concentrating on historical and intellectual perspectives prevailing on both sides. This topic relates to the debates that emerged on the question of freedom of expression in the West (particularly in Europe) and the Muslim world after 9/11. The circumstances subsequently prevailed after 9/11 are also important to understand from both sides of this debate.

The scope of this study ranges from Islam-West relations after 9/11 to the Western concept of freedom of expression and Islamic view of the concept of human freedom as a whole. The changing nature of relations between the Muslim world and the West have been analyzed following the circumstances that led to the outbreak of such debate. Significant space has been given to the scenario in which this debate emerged along with its depth and reasons as described by the scholars. Detailed account of Muslim reaction to the Western concept of freedom of expression is incorporated with description of Islamic concept of freedom of expression.

It is important to note that this book tries to focus on the Muslim-specific freedom of expression debates in Europe and Muslim reaction. This is why the many incidents and controversies in the Muslim world are not examined. Legislation in the Muslim world is surveyed to have an idea of the Muslim conception of freedom of expression, freedom of religion, and blasphemy since they are claimed to be derived from Islamic laws. This survey also gives a compact, but interesting, sense of both similarity and diversity in the Muslim world about these concepts. The word "Muslim" is carefully chosen instead of "Islamic" to reflect laws and ideologies existing in the Muslim world and not what is enshrined in Islam as a religion. This is to avoid conflicting debates within different sects and schools of thought in Islam that are extremely lengthy and could have caused confusion and incoherence. Intellectual debates within the Muslim world are also overlooked for the same reason, but it does not mean that there is nothing to write about or that details are not available or unimportant. Instead, that is a complete topic to study independently and incorporation of such themes in this book would need much extension and explanation that would ultimately distract us from the main topic of study. The study generally covers the time period between September 11, 2001 and 2021.

Why Freedom of Expression? Why Not Free Speech?

Historical and intellectual debate on the definitional aspects of freedom of expression/speech can be seen in chapter 3, but a relevant question could be: Why have I chosen the phrase "expression" and not "freedom of speech" or "free speech," etc.?

In this book, I take the word "expression" in the sense which is more comprehensive than just speech. Although we will see in the coming chapters that freedom of expression and freedom of speech or free speech are interchangeably used everywhere but when we talk about religion, a head covering, face covering, cross, or kippah, can be an expression. We will have to consider all such forms of religious expression, too, before commencing any debate on the freedom of expression. This is important because these kinds of expressions have generated much controversy in the West, and Europe in particular, then just "speech."

Other connotation is the form of expression that sparked debate and controversy when we talk about Muslims in the West or specifically Europe. Major controversies did not arise from a speech or a piece of writing. The forms of expression were cartoons and films that exacerbated the debate around freedom of expression and Muslims in Europe.

What Sort of Debate: Historical? Intellectual? Legal or Religious?

The major debate throughout the dissertation is contemporary. The main focus is on the circumstances that emerged after 9/11. Subsequent events that led to the controversies, acts of violence, and protests are taken into account with a prime focus on the Jyllands-Posten cartoon controversy, the Charlie Hebdo cartoons, and the following terror attacks and Dutch film resulting in Muslim anger.

Historical evolution of the core concepts relating to freedom of expression are incorporated with reference to the definitional aspects and chronological chain of events.

Intellectual aspects of the debate are also given space from Socrates to modern times on different ideologies, concepts, and theories. Theoretical debates over the centuries shall be included related to Western concepts while Islamic injunctions on relevant topics are also discussed.

A significant portion of research is based on legal connotations of different concepts. Freedom of expression and religion in supranational laws, treaties, charters, and covenants forms part of research on the one hand while on the other hand, national laws related to blasphemy are discussed in detail both in Europe and the Muslim world. A detailed account of the provisions on freedom of expression and religion in the constitutions of European and Muslim countries is present in the study.

Islamic religious law governing freedom of expression and religion as well as blasphemy and apostasy is briefly discussed, while more space is given to national laws of relevant Muslim countries to keep the debate current and alive.

What is Meant by Europe in the Research?

More or less fifty sovereign states are counted part of Europe, but this research is centered on countries that are important in terms of their population, geography, demography (i.e., significant Muslim population), and/or being part of any major controversy.

Figure 0.1. Political map of Europe.

Source: https://www.nationsonline.org/oneworld/europe_map.htm

Certain countries are included because of specific incidents and/or laws pointing toward Muslim expression. Almost all of Western Europe, Scandinavia, and part of Central Europe remains a point of focus given this criterion. For example, few states are mentioned while discussing relevant laws regarding freedom of expression and religion criteria being their role in controversy, Muslim population, or important laws, etc.

What is Meant by Muslim World in the Research?

The Organization of Islamic Cooperation (OIC) comprises fifty-seven countries out of which fifty are estimated to be Muslim-majority nations. Those nations as per majority of Muslim population in 2021 are shown in table 0.1.

Table 0.1. Muslim Majority Countries 2021

No.	*Country*	*Muslim Population*	*Population in 2021*	*Muslim Percentage*
1.	Indonesia	229,000,000	276,361,783	87.20
2.	Pakistan	200,400,000	225,199,937	96.50
3.	Bangladesh	153,700,000	166,303,498	90.40
4.	Egypt	87,500,000	104,258,327	83.92
5.	Iran	82,500,000	85,028,759	97.02
6.	Turkey	79,850,000	85,042,738	93.89
7.	Algeria	41,240,913	44,616,624	92.43
8.	Sudan	39,585,777	44,909,353	88.14
9.	Iraq	38,465,864	41,179,350	93.41
10.	Morocco	37,930,989	37,344,795	99.00
11.	Afghanistan	34,836,014	39,835,428	87.51
12.	Saudi Arabia	31,878,000	35,340,683	97.10
13.	Yemen	27,784,498	30,490,640	91.12
14.	Uzbekistan	26,550,000	33,935,763	78.23
15.	Niger	21,101,926	25,130,817	83.96
16.	Syria	16,700,000	18,275,702	93.00
17.	Senegal	15,112,721	17,196,301	87.88
18.	Kazakhstan	13,158,672	18,994,962	70.20
19.	Burkina Faso	12,141,769	21,497,096	61.50
20.	Tunisia	11,190,000	11,935,766	99.80
21.	Somalia	10,978,000	16,359,504	67.10
22.	Guinea	10,563,171	13,497,244	89.10
23.	Jordan	10,165,577	10,269,021	98.20
24.	Malaysia	20,063,50	32,776,19	63.00
25.	Mali	17,508,39	20,855,73	83.95
26.	Azerbaijan	9,735,074	10,223,342	95.22
27.	Chad	9,183,207	16,914,985	58.00
28.	Tajikistan	7,621,700	9,749,627	78.17
29.	Libya	6,551,871	6,958,532	97.00
30.	Sierra Leone	6,067,706	8,141,343	78.60

(continued)

Table 0.1. *(continued)*

No.	*Country*	*Muslim Population*	*Population in 2021*	*Muslim Percentage*
31.	Turkmenistan	4,830,000	6,117,924	78.94
32.	Kyrgyzstan	4,679,438	6,628,356	80.00
33.	United Arab Emirates	6,251,627	9,991,089	72.00
34.	Palestine	4,298,000	5,222,748	97.50
35.	Mauritania	4,161,925	4,775,119	99.00
36.	Lebanon	3,519,743	6,769,146	57.70
37.	Oman	4,633,752	5,223,375	85.90
38.	Kuwait	2,175,684	2,916,467	74.60
39.	Gambia	2,002,743	2,486,945	95.70
40.	Bosnia and Herzegovina	1,955,084	3,263,466	50.70
41.	Kosovo	1,823,657	1,907,592	95.60
42.	Albania	1,797,645	2,872,933	58.80
43.	Qatar	1,566,786	2,930,528	77.50
44.	Bahrain	1,063,239	1,748,296	73.70
45.	Djibouti	857,496	1,002,187	97.00
46.	Comoros	807,204	888,451	98.30
47.	Western Sahara	599,633	661,875	99.40
48.	Maldives	386,193	543,617	98.40
49.	Brunei	355,045	441,532	78.80
50.	Mayotte	253,439	279,515	97.00

Source: https://worldpopulationreview.com

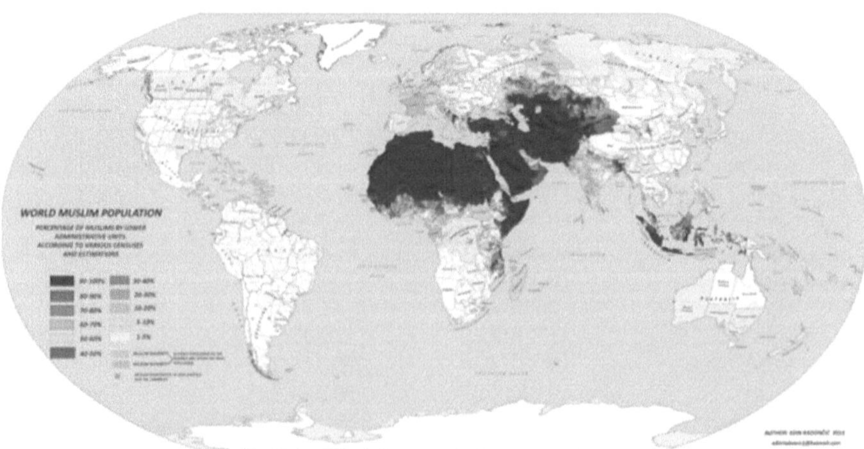

Figure 0.2. Muslim majority countries.

Source: https://www.nationsonline.org/oneworld/map/World-Muslim-Population-map.htm

Selection of Muslim countries among these is done based on four factors:

- Muslim population and its dominance
- Mention of Islam in the constitution
- Blasphemy laws
- Standing in the Muslim world

Few countries are large in Muslim population but are not Muslim-majority nations (e.g., India), some countries have a dominant large Muslim population but do not have strict blasphemy laws (e.g., Sudan), and certain countries have a large dominant Muslim population but are not generally considered crucial and/or instrumental in the Muslim world.

Chapter One

Controversies Regarding Freedom of Expression and Muslims in Europe

THE 9/11 ATTACK AND AFTERMATH

The West blames Al-Qaeda for the 9/11 attacks and its media largely relies, besides other evidence, on a statement from Osama bin Laden called Al-Qaeda's Second Fatwa to prove this claim. In a subsequent TV interview, Osama bin Laden can be seen reiterating fatwa, that according to him, the Islamic scholars have maintained a consensus throughout Islamic history that if Muslim states are under attack by enemies, jihad becomes an individual duty rather than a state declaration.[1] In response, US president George W. Bush declared a "crusade" after the attacks by stating "this crusade, this war on terrorism." He also declared that this war on terror "is going to take a while."[2]

This declaration led many people, especially Muslims, around the globe to the immediate conclusion that the US-led war on terror was against Muslims. Even the American media perceived the same.[3] Europe, on the other hand, got alarmed by this declaration and immediate perception in the media that this "crusade" could lead the world to a "clash of civilizations."[4] The fears were not baseless. Within a week after the attacks, the American media started reporting hate crimes against Muslims, South Asians, and Middle Easterners living in the United States.[5] This was amid the fact that the American Muslims unanimously condemned the attacks, offered condolences, and expressed solidarity with the American people and norms, and showed respect for the law of the land. Attacks were condemned by Muslim leaders, groups, scholars, and media throughout the world too.[6] But Europe also followed the American course in targeting Muslims in particular and media started highlighting such cases within days after 9/11.[7]

These circumstances exacerbated the debate on Islam-West tensions and the term "Islamophobia" was widely used. Even the Secretary General of the

United Nations stated that this terminology was necessary as a way to address the "increasingly widespread bigotry."[8] Throughout Europe and North America, Islam was seen as the sole powerful resistance against freedom, democratic values, and the Judeo-Christian heritage. Scholars noted that "Islamophobia is a 'phobia' of multiculturalism" and the unsettled multicultural effect that Islam, by using its "transcultural processes," can have in Europe and the West.[9]

Western scholars also compared Islamophobia to anti-Semitism and said its effects on Muslims were the same as anti-Semitism on Jews. They termed it "a new social cancer" and called it a sort of discrimination having the basis in religion and/or race also accompanying hate speech.[10] It was also widely regarded that rising Islamophobia was a violation of human rights as one author termed it while also calling it a "threat to social cohesion" no matter if it comes in the form of routine discrimination on the basis of racism or takes more violent turns outside of daily life.[11]

MUSLIMS AND FREEDOM OF EXPRESSION IN THE NETHERLANDS

By the end of 2021, Islam was the second largest religion after Christianity in mostly irreligious Netherlands, with a share of 5.2 percent of the population.[12] An unfavorable environment for Muslims was already present in society prior to the 9/11 attacks as 45 percent of the population saw Muslims with negativity. This ratio rose to 95 percent after the attacks.[13] By the time 9/11 happened, the Dutch nation was already polarized on the issue of Muslim immigrants and in the coming years several right-wing politicians were asking for tougher immigration laws while blaming Muslims for their lack of integration into Dutch society.[14]

On May 6, 2002, Dutch politician Wilhelmus Simon Petrus (Pim) Fortuyn was assassinated in Hilversum by the thirty-three-year-old environmental rights activist Volkert van der Graaf. He said that he killed Fortuyn to protect "Dutch Muslims from persecution" while confessing to the first political assassination in the Netherlands in four hundred years. He said, "I confess to the shooting. He was an ever-growing danger who would affect many people in society. I saw it as a danger. I hoped that I could solve it myself."[15]

Fortuyn had become a symbol of anti-immigrant, anti-Muslim politics in the Netherlands after 9/11. Leading an openly gay lifestyle, Fortuyn used to call immigrants a "mess" and Islam "backward."[16] Fortuyn's killer got eighteen years in prison, but his death changed the sociopolitical landscape of the country toward more anti-immigrant and anti-Muslims subsequently giving rise to politicians like Geert Wilders.

DUTCH FILM AND CARTOON CONTROVERSIES

The first major controversy regarding freedom of expression and Muslims emerged when Dutch journalist and filmmaker Theodoor (Theo) van Gogh released a film titled *Submission: Part 1* on August 29, 2004. Van Gogh was born on July 23, 1957, in The Hague and became a stage manager and actor after dropping out of law school and later contributed regularly to the local free newspaper *Dutch Metro*. A friend and supporter of Fortuyn, van Gogh has been described as "enfant terrible," "a clearly ambiguous figure," and well-known to pass "derogatory statements against Muslims and Jews." He also used to call himself an "intellectual terrorist."[17] He wrote his last book titled *Allah Weet Het Beter* (Allah Knows Best) in 2003, which has been described as mockingly critical to Islam.[18] Shortly before his assassination, van Gogh was said to have completed a film on the deceased politician Pim Fortuyn.[19]

It is also reported that van Gogh was such a failure being a political columnist that "almost every newspaper of the country" fired him. He would love to cross the line of free speech toward hate-mongering and used to call conservative Muslims "goat-fuckers." On August 29, 2004, Theo van Gogh released his eleven-minute film titled *Submission: Part 1* written by Ayaan Hirsi Ali, a female Somali critic of Islam living in the Netherlands and elected to parliament. The subject matter of the film deals with the treatment and perception of women in Islam and was criticized for its "laziness as both art and protest" being a "morsel of glib effrontery."[20] Hirsi Ali and van Gogh both were also accused of plagiarism with accusations of not mentioning their source of inspiration in the film.[21] After the film's release, van Gogh received death threats but refused to accept any protection saying that "nobody kills the village idiot."[22]

On November 2, 2004, Mohammed Bouyeri, a twenty-six-year-old Moroccan-Dutch man shot van Gogh in Amsterdam, cut his throat, and stabbed a letter to his chest with a knife. The letter was addressed to Ayan Hirsi Ali claiming that Islam will be victorious and her "intellectual terrorism" would fail. Police followed the killer, shot him in leg, and arrested him.[23] He was later sentenced to life in prison on July 26, 2005, by a Dutch court as he took no defense. After the killing of Fortuyn, the assassination of van Gogh further polarized Dutch society and made the right-wingers much stronger. Tolerance for immigrants, especially Muslims, dipped sharply as it was deemed "cowardice" even by close friends of van Gogh.[24] The murder of van Gogh also resulted in attacks on mosques and counterattacks on churches in the Netherlands.[25] The killing of van Gogh gave more rise to right-wing politics in the Netherlands and politicians like Geert Wilders rose to prominence.

Wilders left the VVD party in September 2004 when the European Union started negotiations to include Turkey and founded his Party for Freedom

(Partij voor de Vrijheid) in 2006.[26] *Time* magazine described him as the "Dutch Donald Trump":

> Wilders gained the nickname of the "Dutch Trump" for his ability to court controversy, his effective use of social media, his demonization of immigrants, and his peroxide blonde bouffant hairstyle. Now it seems like he is lagging in the polls due to what is being described as the "Trump effect."[27]

Wilders declared at the beginning of his political career that he hated Islam and wanted "end to mosque building and Muslim immigration." In the 2010 elections, his party reached twenty-four seats after winning only nine in previous elections and vowed to "ban [the] Koran" and "tax . . . headscarves."

On March 27, 2008, Wilders released his fifteen-minute film titled *Fitna* through which he wanted to warn the West about a "dangerous and intolerant" religion called Islam. The Dutch prime minister termed this an offense while stating that he rejected this interpretation of equating Islam with violence.[28] UN Secretary General Ban Ki-Moon labeled the film "offensively anti-Islamic," and Wilders had to remove one of the controversial cartoons of *Jyllands-Posten* from the film after the Dutch Union of Journalists announced legal action on behalf of cartoonist Kurt Westergaard whose permission was not taken to use the cartoon.[29]

On February 12, 2009, Wilders was sent back to the Netherlands when he tried to enter the United Kingdom because a ban was placed on his entry due to his film. However, in March 2010, he was not only permitted to enter the United Kingdom but was also allowed to screen his film in the House of Lords. A lot of citizens in the Netherlands released their own short videos to apologize for Wilders's move and to state that views in the film are not of the Dutch nation and state. An advertisement by producer and president of the Another Jewish Voice foundation, Harry de Winter, appeared in the newspaper *Volkskrant* on March 17, 2008, saying that Wilders would have been accused of anti-Semitism had this film been about Jews. The advertisement reads: "If Wilders would have said the same about Jews (and the Old Testament) as what he is now spouting about Muslims (and the Koran), he would have long since been banned and convicted for anti-Semitism."

Figure 1.1. Advertisement by Harry de Winter in *Volkskrant*.

Source: https://mronline.org/wp-content/uploads/2017/01/harry_de_winter_ad.jpg

Arnoud Van Doorn, who was a leader of Wilders's party and had helped in the making of the film *Fitna* announced to convert to Islam in early 2013 leaving Wilders's party. He also announced to produce a film in praise of Islam and the Prophet Muhammad later.[30]

In 2018, another long-standing right-hand aide of Wilders converted to Islam while writing a book against it. Joram van Klaveren revealed this in February 2019 and his book was eventually converted into a book favoring Islam with the title *Apostate: From Christianity to Islam in the Time of Secular Terror.* Klaveren called it a "religious homecoming" and parted ways with Wilders. Islam also continued to grow in the Netherlands despite Wilders's campaign against it.[31] At the end of 2019, Wilders announced that he was going to revive his controversial drawing contest tweeting that "freedom of speech must prevail."[32]

MUSLIMS AND FREEDOM OF EXPRESSION IN DENMARK

It is very important to understand that the cartoons depicting the Prophet Muhammad did not appear suddenly in a Danish newspaper without having any historical, political, or cultural context. There had been a debate on the status of immigrants and particularly Muslims and their ideologies in Danish society, politics, and media before *Jyllands-Posten* attempted such publication. Unfortunately, this debate was biased against immigrants and especially Muslims. Several analyses show that Islam and Muslims were being presented negatively in Danish media before the publication of such cartoons and this was an ultimate result of what had been going on.[33]

There were approximately 256,000 Muslims in Denmark by 2020, constituting 4.4 percent of the population.[34] Since the 1990s, there has been debate about Denmark being an Islamophobic country, which intensified after 9/11, the active Danish role in Iraq's invasion, and ultimately the cartoon controversy. Elections were called just after 9/11 and Muslim immigrants were part of heated debate during electioneering. Muslim organizations demanded meeting with the Danish prime minister to discuss increasing difficulties to which the prime minister initially nodded then declined. Elections were held on November 20, 2001, and the new government introduced stricter measures to curb illegal immigration that exacerbated the existing debate on Muslims and immigrants, increasing polarization, and the separation of religion and state, etc.[35]

In 2007, after the *Jyllands-Posten* cartoon controversy, hijab-wearing Muslim female Asmaa Abdol-Hamid tried to get candidature of the Red-Green Alliance for a Copenhagen seat. She failed the attempt and rather a debate was caused about her initiative and whether a hijab-clad woman can run for candidature or not. Even one MP compared her to the Nazis.[36]

THE *JYLLANDS-POSTEN* PUBLICATION

In 2005, the year *Jyllands-Posten* published such cartoons, Muslims constituted 5 percent of the total population of 5.4 million with a number of 270,000. At that time, Muslims were already finding it hard to get housing and jobs in Denmark and only a few of them had citizenship.[37] Denmark was experiencing racial tensions when cartoons appeared, and in 1997 a survey conducted by *Jyllands-Posten* revealed that Muslims were seen as a threat by half of the Danish population. By 2002, the Far Right anti-immigrant Danish People's Party (DPP) was already present in national parliament as the third largest group. The DPP already had a very hard stance against Muslims terming them "at a lower stage of civilization."[38] It was also observed that there was a "we" feeling of native Danes against Muslims residing in their country and they were told to leave Denmark in response to any argument they used to give in their favor.[39]

Paper's Background and Views on Islam and Muslims

Founded on October 2, 1871, the Danish Newspaper *Morgenavisen Jyllands-Posten* means *The Morning Newspaper "The Jutland Post"*. It describes itself as "Denmark's International Newspaper" and claims to be country's largest newspaper both in its printed version and on the internet with a readership of more than 355,000 people on weekdays and 483,000 on Sundays.

On March 20, 2002, while passing an order by majority vote, the Danish Press Council expressed criticism of *Jyllands-Posten* for expressing racial discrimination against Somalis. It said that the newspaper "acted contrary to the ethics of journalism."[40] In April 2003, the paper refused to publish cartoons of Jesus. A note from the Sunday editor Jens Kaiser, who thought that "they will provoke an outcry," also feared that this publication "would offend some readers" although he was not sure about many but was suspicious about some readers who would not take this positively and get angry.[41]

While finding *Jyllands-Posten* as one of the foremost negative portrayers of ethnic minorities, the European Network Against Racism (ENAR) noted a continuous propaganda against Islam in Danish media. ENAR noted in its 2004 report that many writers in the Danish media, along with several commentators and academics, were misusing their freedom of expression and writing whatever they liked. They were also noted to pass derogatory remarks frequently in their writings while using a language that insulted Muslims. The report mentioned Lars Hedegaard as a so-called historian who regards himself an expert in dealing with anything and everything having any connection to Islam and Muslims. The report further noted the writings of *Jyllands-Posten* and said his statements to that right-wing newspaper are quite evident about his mental state with regard to a particular religion and its followers.

The ENAR report then quotes Hedegaard from his publication in *Jyllands-Posten* on August 1, 2004, in which he tags Islam as "more totalitarian than Nazism." Hedegaard wrote that every corner of a follower's life is altered and monitored by Islam be it dressing or how to eat.[42]

In 2005, *Jyllands-Posten* started running a number of stories that were focused on imams having radical tendencies based in the Aarhus area. The paper had a particular pinpoint toward two imams who had made their headquarters in Gellerup.[43] The newspaper also advocated Israeli actions against Palestinians and wrote in 2009 that Hamas and Palestinians are responsible for "putting Israel's existence at stake." The paper also advocated the right of Israel to defend itself against any threat posed by Palestinians in whatever manner it deemed fit. The paper appreciated those international actors who did not condemn Israeli aggression on Gaza and termed that silence as "just a tribute to Israel." It also blamed Hamas in the same piece of hiding behind civilians to carry out attacks on Israel. The paper tried to justify civilian deaths as a result of Israeli bombings and wrote that after all that is a war against Palestinians, and civilian losses always occur during wars. The paper said that Israel is fighting against "blind radicalism" and predicted that this radicalism can soon be seen in many European capitals too.[44]

Amin and Mona Sheikh Stories

In 1997, a ten-year-old Muslim boy named Amin denied to bathing in a same-sex communal shower after swimming classes in Frederikssund town. His three elder siblings had negotiated an arrangement with the same school administration while studying there to bathe ten minutes before everyone else. Other parents did not raise any objection to such arrangement but at Amin's time, the headmaster denied such facility saying that this is not forbidden in Islam to bathe with others. Amin's parents took stance that the headmaster would not define their religion and they had to withdraw Amin and his elder brother from school as a result.[45] *Jyllands-Posten* extensively covered the story while developing "face and figure of an enemy" calling Muslims "evil" who were not desiring to integrate and live in the Middle Ages being "happy with Afghani conditions." The paper repeatedly used words "abomination," "darkening," and "Middle Ages-like" for Muslims.[46] As a result of this continued negative coverage, Amin became an unwanted child who got stigmatized with having an unhygienic lifestyle and as a result got expelled from school.[47]

In the spring of 2001, twenty-three-year-old Mona Sheikh was among three young politicians with Pakistani parents who were running for candidature in the Social-Liberal Party (Det Radikale Venstre). Their integrity and aspirations came under attack and Mona Sheikh in particular had to answer so many questions on media related to Sharia and the death penalty in Islam, etc. This ultimately led to Mona withdrawing her candidature and country, having a debate questioning young Pakistanis with accusations of trying to destabilize democracy, and altering the parliamentary system in Denmark.[48] The Danish media extensively covered Mona and in fact two journalists quoted her completely opposite on the death penalty. *Jyllands-Posten* reported more than any publication on the issue and the language on Islam and Muslims was no different from what was later used during the cartoon controversy. During this period, the newspaper was publishing titles like "Islam's dirty face" (*Islams beskidte ansigt*, May 22) and "Forces of darkness" (*Mørkets kræfter*, May 27). All this reflected immediately after the cartoon controversy in official statements as Danish Minister for Culture Brian Mikkelsen said on September 25, 2005, that the Muslim culture is having "Middle age norms" as well as "anti-democratic ways of thinking."[49]

Publication of Cartoons and Subsequent Reaction

On September 30, 2005, *Jyllands-Posten* published twelve cartoons related to Islam while most depicted the Prophet Muhammad. The caption given to those cartoons was "The Face of Muhammad" and Culture Editor Flemming Rose later wrote that it was between "Islam and the secular" while mentioning "Western societies rooted in Christianity." He argued that some Muslims "demand a special position and consideration" while their religious feelings are "incompatible with secular democracy and freedom of speech."[50]

Another Danish newspaper, *Berlingske Tidende*, regarded progovernment, condemned the publication of the twelve cartoons by *Jyllands-Posten* calling it an "unnecessary irresponsible provocation."[51] On January 1, 2006, the Danish prime minister condemned any "expression, action or indication" that "attempt to demonize groups of people" saying that no one can be hurt on the basis of their "religion or ethnic background," but also reiterated Denmark's commitment to freedom of speech.[52] The situation worsened when a Norwegian Christian newspaper, *Magazinet*, reprinted the cartoons on January 10 and in French, German, Italian, and Spanish newspapers the very next day, which added to Muslim anger.[53]

In Europe, besides protests by Muslims, Belarus handed over a criminal sentence of three years in jail to a newspaper editor on January 18, 2008. Aleksandr Sdvizhkov, editor of the weekly newspaper *Zgoda* (*Consensus*) was convicted for "incitement of religious hatred" after he reprinted the *Jyllands-Posten* cartoons in February 2006.[54]

On January 29, 2006, *Jyllands-Posten* published an open letter to the "honored citizens of the Kingdom of Saudi Arabia" in which the affair was "regretted" without tendering an apology.[55] The next day, *Jyllands-Posten* issued an apology to the "honorable citizens of the Muslim world" for offending them, but not for publishing the cartoons. The editor however emphasized that the paper's position on the publication had not changed as such and said that if apologizing for printing the cartoons would mean that the decision is now in the hands of "dictators in the Middle East" to tell us what to be published in our newspaper "that is of course totally unacceptable."[56]

Flemming Rose, the culture editor who published the cartoons, described the background of the publication in an opinion piece appearing in *The Washington Post* in February 2006, stating that while we talk about issues concerning Islam, "several incidents of self-censorship" took place in Europe and the reason behind that was "widening fears and feelings of intimidation." He wrote that he commissioned the cartoons in response to this threat. In the same article, Rose defended his act and claimed that Islam was treated just like the cartoonists treat other religions. He further claimed that Muslims were not demonized or stereotyped in any way by those cartoons.[57]

MUSLIMS AND FREEDOM OF EXPRESSION IN FRANCE

In 2006, the weekly magazine *Charlie Hebdo*, printed a cartoon of the Prophet Muhammad. At that time, too, like today, France had the largest Muslim population in Western Europe with 5 to 6 million adherents constituting 8 to 9.6 percent of the 62.3 million French citizens.[58] But at the same time, when riots erupted in Paris in 2005, many French believed that Muslim immigrants were behind it.[59]

It is also noteworthy that the Muslim headscarf controversy started in France in 1989, the first of its kind in Europe, when three female Muslim students refused to remove their headscarves and consequently expelled from a middle school in Creil on September 18. The same thing happened the next January with three other Muslim females in Noyon. Parents of one girl filed defamation against the school principal. Against this, teachers in a Nantua middle school went on strike and the government, in both instances, took stance in favor of secularism in educational institutions while urging to judge such issues on a case-by-case basis. In Mantes-la-Jolie, students at Saint-Exupéry High School staged a gathering in October favoring veils in the classrooms. Twenty-four veiled girls were expelled from school the next month as well as from Faidherbe High School in Lille. More or less one hundred girls were expelled or suspended from schools between 1994 and 2003 for wearing headscarves and almost half won cases in local courts against this action.[60] By late 2003, a sense of alienation in Muslims was such that then President Jacques Chirac had to address it: "I share the feeling of incomprehension, of disarray and sometimes even of revolt by those young French people—immigrants by origin—whose job applications go into the garbage because of the sound of their names, and who are too often faced with discrimination when they want to find housing or even get into a place of recreation."[61] But at the same time, the then Interior Minister Nicolas Sarkozy passed on a clear message to Muslims and said, "There are no rights without duties, and if the Muslims of France have the same rights as other believers, they have the same duties."[62]

It was claimed by *The Washington Post* in 2008 that Muslims were merely 12 percent of the French population but prisons in France were full with 60 to -70 percent Muslim prisoners.[63] The situation kept changing and by 2010 it was evident that French society was expressing religious bias against Muslims.[64] France placed an official ban on face coverings in public places in April 2011 and in July 2013 riots broke out in Trappes when the police arrested a man who assaulted them after police tried to check his wife in veil.[65]

In October 2012, the French newspaper *Le Figaro* shared results of a survey about images of Islam being "sharply deteriorated" in France with an irreversible "negative coverage."[66] The next month, the UK newspaper *The Independent* reported that France was having a "proud secularist tradition," which is "hijacked" by right-wing media, which was attacking Muslims. *The Independent* cited an example of French magazine *Le Point* that published a picture of veiled woman with the heading "Brazen Islam." On this, then French interior minister said that "it expresses a reality" that he is always shocked to see a fully veiled woman instead. *The Independent* observed that to stigmatize Islam and Muslims was "now fine for the whole political class" in France.[67]

CHARLIE HEBDO PUBLICATIONS AND ATTACKS

Magazine's Background

Charlie Hebdo was first published in 1969. "*Charlie*" is an homage to the cartoon character Charlie Brown while "*Hebdo*" is a shortened version of the word "*hebdomadair*e," which means "weekly" in French. Soon after its birth, the magazine was labelled as "dumb and nasty," which was adopted as its official slogan.[68]

It was first published by workers of a monthly magazine entitled *Hara-Kiri*, which was banned after mocking the death of former French president Charles de Gaulle as, "Tragic dance at Colombey [de Gaulle's home]–one dead" in its headline. The magazine never had good numbers and remained ceased for a decade after 1981 due to lack of resources.[69] Having a "vocally left, anti-authoritarian, anti-religious, and anti-institutional" stance, *Charlie Hebdo* remained under criticism for maintaining a long tradition of "intentionally controversial and provocative cartoons and covers." It also had a history of publishing cartoons mocking Muslims, especially after 9/11.[70]

Depictions of the Prophet Muhammad in 2006

On February 8, 2006, *Charlie Hebdo* printed a front-page cartoon of the Prophet Muhammad under the title "Mohammed overwhelmed by fundamentalists," while inside, twelve of the controversial *Jyllands-Posten* cartoons were reproduced with some more of its own design. This tripled the sales of the magazine amid support from the politicians who were critical of its content with the exception of French president Jacques Chirac, who said that one should avoid everything that can hurt someone else, "in particular religious convictions," he said.[71]

In February 2007, French Islamic groups took *Charlie Hebdo* to court for "publicly abusing a group of people because of their religion," but its magazine editor was cleared of accusations by the court ruling that he had rights to satire Islamic extremism and while one cartoon maybe offensive, Muslims were not offended deliberately.[72] In August 2008, a satirical column by Maurice Siné, who was writing for *Charlie Hebdo* for two decades was termed anti-Semitic by the magazine and Siné was fired after he refused to tender an apology.

The Guardian criticized *Charlie Hebdo* editor Val and wrote that he was the one who, while defending freedom of expression, "took the controversial decision to re-publish" *Jyllands-Posten* cartoons and now asked Siné to apologize for his "offensive" piece.[73] Siné went to the court and won a 40,000 Euro judgment against his dismissal on the issue.[74]

Cartoon Published in 2011 and 2012

Charlie Hebdo defended itself for publishing cartoons in 2006 by publishing a letter and on November 1, 2011, it published a caricature of the Prophet Muhammad while announcing he would be the magazine's "editor-in-chief" for next issue. The following day, the magazine's offices were destroyed by firebombing leaving no one hurt.[75]

On September 19, 2012, the Prophet Muhammad was again depicted in a manner that prompted the French government (which had urged the magazine not to publish cartoons) to close its embassies and schools in twenty countries fearing Muslim backlash. These cartoons were published just after release of a controversial film in the United States about Islam, and French authorities had banned any Muslim protests against the film. This timing of publication was condemned by French politicians and the media terming that "irresponsible, inopportune, and imbecilic." The chief of police requested the editor to "think again," which he refused and French prime minister Jean-Marc Ayrault criticized the cartoons and similar "excesses." The French foreign minister questioned whether it was really intelligent of the weekly "to pour fuel on the fire?"[76] But however, the French government banned any protests against *Charlie Hebdo*.[77]

The French press was divided on the issue when the center-right daily *Le Figaro* termed publication of images "as easy as it is irresponsible" calling it "silly provocations." *Ouest France* warned that it is "very wrong" to engage in a "game of contempt, sarcasm and stigmatization" while "claiming to defend the freedom of expression." *Sud Ouest* wrote that "Charlie Hebdo plays with fire." The *Journal du Centre* asked, "Are these some cartoons too many?" and daily *La Croix* wrote that "fueling the flames . . . leads to offending simple believers" in its editorial titled "Proof by Provocation."[78]

Senior editor of *Charlie Hebdo*, George Biard, once stated that "attacking all religions is the basis of our identity" while another editor and cartoonist named Stéphane Charbonnier, known as Charb, expressed resolve to continue this "until Islam has been rendered as banal as Catholicism."[79] Charbonnier was living under police protection after receiving death threats and was killed on January 7, 2015, in an attack.

The 2015 Firing Incident

On Wednesday, January 7, 2015, *Charlie Hebdo's* front-page featured controversial French author Michel Houellebecq, whose book *Soumission* (*Submission*) was also released on the same day. In 2011, he had described Islam as "the stupidest of all religions" before distancing himself from this statement. His book gathered criticism from French mainstream media, social media, and politicians.[80] The book predicted a France "that is ruled by an Islamic government" and was regarded a milestone in unearthing the increasing negative feelings of non-Muslim French about "immigration and the rise of Islam's influence in society." The same issue of *Charlie Hebdo* carried the cartoon entitled "Still No Attacks in France" in which an Islamist was depicted saying, "Just wait, we have until the end of January to present our New Year's wishes." Minutes before the attack took place, the magazine tweeted a satirical depiction of an ISIS leader giving wishes of Happy New Year.[81]

Later that day, two masked gunmen later known as the brothers Cherif and Said Kouachi, approached the offices of *Charlie Hebdo* in Rue Nicolas-Appert. They opened fire and killed the editor's police bodyguard, editor

Stephane Charbonnier, four other cartoonists, three other editorial staff, and a guest. Police reached the spot and blocked the gunmen's escape when they were leaving the building toward Allee Vert, a narrow street. The gunmen opened fire, riddled the police car's windscreen leaving officers unhurt, and drove south down the Boulevard Richard Lenoir. The gunmen then doubled back on the northern carriageway, got out of the vehicle, and shot police officer Ahmed Merabet on a nearby pavement. One of the attackers got out of the car, shot the injured officer dead at close range, and drove away with his accomplice. The gunmen hijacked a car and disappeared as their car apparently crashed into another vehicle.

Police started searching for the attackers, and during their operation on January 8, a gunman who was said to be linked with the Kouachi brothers, shot dead a policewoman in the southern Paris suburb of Montrouge, injured a man, and escaped. Several people were also taken hostage in eastern Paris by a gunman identified as Amedy Coulibaly who threatened to kill people if the Kouachi brothers were not set free. The Kouachi brothers then robbed a fuel station and took refuge in a building thirty-five kilometers from Paris. On January 9, the two brothers came out of the building, fired at police, and were killed. Soon after this, Coulibaly was shot dead by police, fifteen hostages were freed, and four bodies were found.[82] On January 8, the investigating police commissioner Helric Fredou committed suicide in his office while preparing a report after meeting with a victim's family.[83]

Reaction and the Aftermath

The French government, and those worldwide, condemned the attack. French president François Hollande visited the shooting site and addressed his nation on television saying that "the attack was an attack on all of France and on the ideal of freedom of expression." A day of national mourning was declared on January 8 by the French government. Tens of thousands of people protested across France and in same numbers condemned the attack with #JeSuisCharlie hashtag on social media. Leaders of the United States and the European Union as well as Russia, along with UN Secretary General Ban Ki-moon, expressed solidarity with the victims while condemning the attack.[84]

The attack on *Charlie Hebdo* exacerbated Islamophobia in France and the Far Right took full advantage of that while the Left remained silent or somewhat helpless. Unfortunately, the French government also acted against ordinary Muslims.[85] The leader of the National Front in France, Marine Le Pen, expressed his commitment to "fight the advance of political Islam."[86] There was a debate on whether anyone was "Charlie or not." Policing was demanded for the people who were "not Charlie."[87] Immediately after the *Charlie Hebdo* attack, Muslims were thought to be "incompatible" with French values by the majority of citizens and France was not paying heed to the problems faced by Muslim immigrants.[88]

Reprinting and Aftermath: 2020

On September 1, 2020, France was seeing demonstrations against racism and violation of minority rights when *Charlie Hebdo* republished controversial caricatures on the eve of beginning of the 2015 attack trial.[89] On September 26, an eighteen-year-old Pakistani was arrested for injuring two persons with a meat cleaver near the former offices of *Charlie Hebdo*. This was a time when heated debate was going on in France over immigration and President Macron was expected to present a policy on "separatism" with a particular focus on Islamic radicalism.[90]

On October 16, a teenaged boy of Chechen origin was shot dead by police when he beheaded a history teacher who was said to have showed *Charlie Hebdo* cartoons in the classroom. The Western media reported that French president Emmanuel Macron exploited this incident for his far-right politics and called it an Islamist terror attack. Macron's remarks just days before the incident include:

> Islam is a religion in crisis all over the world today, we don't see it only in our country. In a few days, you can see radical Islamists . . . take control of associations (running mosques) and all their finances. That won't happen again. Fear is about to change sides; Islamists should not be allowed sleep soundly in our country.

After the attack, authorities cracked down on "anything they deemed to be Islamism" displayed in controversial cartoons and on state buildings. Macron was accused of inflating the crisis instead of resolving it. On October 29, three people were attacked in a church in France after *Charlie Hebdo* again decided to print more cartoons earlier that week displaying Muslims.[91] Macron also said that Muslims in France were building a "parallel culture," "Islam is in crisis globally," and announced, "not to renounce caricatures." Macron's government also proposed a harsh law against "Islamist separatism" and all this was met with severe criticism, condemnation, and calls for a boycott of the Muslim world.[92]

NOTES

1. National Commission on Terrorist Attacks, *The 9/11 Commission Report: Final Report of the National Commission on Terrorist Attacks upon the United States* (New York: Norton, 2004), 47.

2. "Remarks by the President upon Arrival, the South Lawn," The White House, September 16, 2001, accessed April 1, 2020, http://georgewbush-whitehouse.archives.gov/news/releases/2001/09/20010916-2.html.

3. Peter Waldman and Hugh Pope, "'Crusade' Reference Reinforces Fears War on Terrorism Is against Muslims," *Wall Street Journal*, September 21, 2001.

4. Peter Ford, "Europe Cringes at Bush 'crusade' Against Terrorists," *Christian Science Monitor*, September 19, 2001.

5. Human Rights Watch, "United States 'We Are Not the Enemy' Hate Crimes against Arabs, Muslims and Those Perceived to be Arab or Muslim after September 11," *Human Rights Watch Report* 14, no. 6 (G), November 2002.

6. "Muslim Groups Decry Attacks," *Washington Times*, September 12, 2001.

7. Chris Allen, *Islamophobia* (New York: Routledge, 2016), 125.

8. Kofi Annan, "Confronting Islamophobia: Education for Tolerance and Understanding," United Nations press release, December 7, 2004.

9. Gabriele Marranci, "Multiculturalism, Islam and the Clash of Civilizations Theory: Rethinking Islamophobia," *Culture and Religion: An Interdisciplinary Journal* 5, no. 1 (2004): 105–17.

10. John L. Esposito, *The Future of Islam* (New York: Oxford University Press, 2010), 197.

11. Ingrid Ramberg, "Islamophobia and Its Consequences on Young People" (published as seminar report by European Youth Centre, Budapest, June 6, 2004), 6.

12. Statistics Netherlands, *The Netherlands in numbers* (The Hague: Statistics Netherlands, 2021), 29.

13. Maurits S. Berger, "The Netherlands," in *The Oxford Handbook of European Islam*, ed. Jocelyne Cesari (Oxford: Oxford University Press, 2014), 196.

14. "Controversial Filmmaker Shot Dead," *Independent*, November 2, 2004.

15. Ambrose Evans-Pritchard and Joan Clements, "Fortuyn Killed 'to Protect Muslims'," *Telegraph*, March 28, 2003.

16. "Dutch Politician Pim Fortuyn Assassinated," *Guardian*, May 6, 2002.

17. Ron Eyerman, *The Assassination of Theo van Gogh: From Social Drama to Cultural Trauma* (Durham and London: Duke University Press, 2008), 8–9.

18. Paul Weller, *A Mirror for Our Times: 'the Rushdie affair' and the Future of Multiculturalism* (London: Bloomsbury Academic, 2009), 158.

19. Marlise Simons, "Dutch Filmmaker, an Islam Critic, Is Killed," *New York Times*, November 3, 2004.

20. Dennis Lim, "The Day I Became a Martyr: Islam Protest Brings Fatal Fatwa," *The Village Voice*, November 9, 2004.

21. Janny Groen, "Hirsi Ali en van Gogh van plagiaat beticht," *de Volkskrant (Amsterdam)*, September 1, 2004.

22. Ayaan Hirsi Ali, *Infidel* (New York: Free Press, 2007), 314.

23. Sasha Polakow-Suransky, *Go Back to Where You Came From* (London: C. Hurst and Company, 2017), 34.

24. Rachel Donadio, "Provocateur's Death Haunts the Dutch," *New York Times*, October 30, 2014.

25. John Hooper, "Italian TV to Screen Dutch Film Despite Muslim Protests Over," *Guardian*, May 11, 2005.

26. James Taranto, "Our Culture Is Better' Champion of Freedom or Anti-Islamic Provocateur? Both.," *Wall Street Journal*, November 29, 2008.

27. Tara John, "What to Know about Geert Wilders, the 'Dutch Trump'," *Time* , March 10, 2017.

28. Gregory Crouch, "Dutch Film against Islam is released on Internet," *New York Times*, March 28, 2008.

29. "Controversial Cartoon Cut from Dutch MP's Film on Islam," *Guardian*, April 1, 2008.

30. Majed Al-Sugairi, "Ex-Islamophobe to Produce Film on Prophet," *Saudi Gazette*, April 22, 2013.

31. "Dutch former anti-Muslim MP Converts to Islam," *The News (Pakistan)*, February 6, 2019.

32. "Geert Wilders Revives Contest for Cartoons That Mock Muhammad," *Guardian*, December 28, 2019.

33. Peter Hervik, *Current Themes in IMER Research: The Danish Muhammad Cartoon Conflict* (Malmo: Malmo University, 2012), 15, 218.

34. Jesper Petersen, *The Making of a Mosque with Female Imams: Serendipities in the Production of Danish Islams* (Leiden: Kolninklijke Brill, 2022), 30–37.

35. Garbi Schmidt, "Denmark," in *Islam in the Nordic and Baltic Countries*, ed. Göran Larsson (London: Routledge, 2009), 45–47.

36. Ibid., 48–49.

37. "Muslims in Europe: Country Guide," BBC.com, December 23, 2005.

38. Peter McGraw and Joel Warner, *The Humor Code: A Global Search for What Makes Things Funny* (New York: Simon and Shuster, 2014), 138.

39. Peter Hervik, *The Annoying Difference: The Emergence of Danish Neonationalism, Neoracism, and Populism in the Post-1989 World* (New York: Berghahn Books, 2011), 277.

40. "Order of the Press Council in Case No. 23/2002" April 10, 2002.

41. Gwladys Fouché, "Danish Paper Rejected Jesus Cartoons," *Guardian*, February 6, 2006.

42. Bashy Quraishy and Jean o'Connor, *ENAR Shadow Report 2004 Denmark* (European Network Against Racism, 2004), 23.

43. Pernille Ammitzbøll and Lorenzo Vidino, "After the Danish Cartoon Controversy," *Middle East Quarterly* 14, no. 1 (Winter 2007): 3–11.

44. "Leder: Israel i Gaza," *Jyllands-Posten*, January 6, 2009.

45. Sidsel Vive Jensen and Lene Kühle, "School Islam: Lived Religion in the Context of a Secular Public Institution," in *Everyday Lived Islam in Europe* (New York: Routledge, 2013), 110.

46. Githa Hariharan, *Almost Home: Finding a Place in the World from Kashmir to New York* (New York: Restless Books, 2014), 226.
47. *Current Themes in IMER Research*, 23.
48. Mikkel Rytter, *Family Upheaval: Generation, Mobility, and Relatedness among Pakistani Migrants in Denmark* (New York: Berghahn Books, 2013), 46.
49. *Current Themes in IMER Research*, 26–27.
50. Flemming Rose, "Muhammad's Face," *Jyllnads-Posten*, September 30, 2005.
51. *Current Themes in IMER Research*, 17.
52. Ole Riis, "Religious Pluralism in a Local and Global Perspective: Images of the Prophet Muhammad Seen in a Danish and a Global Context," in *Religion, Globalization, and Culture* (Leiden: Brill, 2007), 435.
53. "Muslim Cartoon Row Timeline," BBC.com, February 19, 2006.
54. Carl Bernstein, *Attacks on the Press in 2008: A Worldwide Survey by the Committee to Protect Journalists* (New York: Committee to Protect Journalists, 2009), 164.
55. "Cartoon Paper Justifies Itself to Saudis," *Brussels Journal*, January 29, 2006.
56. "Danish Paper Apologizes. Dutch Cartoon on Its Way," *Brussels Journal*, January 31, 2006.
57. Flemming Rose, "Why I Published Those Cartoons," *Washington Post*, February 19, 2006.
58. "Muslims in Europe: Country Guide," BBC.com.
59. Olivier Roy, "The Nature of the French Riots" (paper presented at the Riots in France, Social Science Research Council, New York, 2005).
60. Nicky Jones, "Beneath the Veil: Muslim Girls and Islamic Headscarves in Secular France," *Macquarie Law Journal* 9 (2009): 47–52.
61. Elaine Sciolino, "Chirac Wants Religious Attire Banned in Public Schools," *New York Times*, December 17, 2003.
62. "Muslim Leader Says France Has Right to Prohibit Head Scarves," *New York Times*, December 31, 2003.
63. Molly Moore, "In France, Prisons Filled with Muslims," *Washington Post*, April 29, 2008.
64. Claire Adida, David Laitin, and Marie-Anne Valfort, *Les Français musulmans sont-ils discriminés dans leur propre pays? Une étude expérimentale sur le marché du travail* (Paris: French-American Foundation & Sciences Po, 2010).
65. "Riots in France: Trouble in Trappes," *The Economist*, July 27, 2013.
66. "L'image de l'Islam en France," IFoP pour Le Figaro, October 2012.
67. Marie Dhumieres, "When Did Islamophobic Attacks Become the Norm for the French Media?" *Independent*, November 7, 2012.
68. Oliver Duggan, "The History of Charlie Hebdo, Bastion of French Satire," *Telegraph*, January 7, 2015.
69. "Charlie Hebdo and its Place in French Journalism," BBC.com.
70. "In Solidarity with Charlie Hebdo, Here Are 16 of Their Most Controversial Cartoons," DeadState.org, January 7, 2015.
71. Jonathan Turley, "The Biggest Threat to French Free Speech Isn't Terrorism. It's the Government," *Washington Post*, January 8, 2015.

72. Craig S. Smith, "French Court Rules for Newspaper That Printed Muhammad Cartoons," *New York Times*, March 23, 2007.

73. Jason Burke, '"Anti-Semitic' Satire Divides Liberal Paris," *Guardian*, August 3, 2008.

74. Imen Neffati, "Anti-Sociologisme, Zionism, and Islamophobia in Philippe Val's Charlie Hebdo," *French Cultural Studies* 32, no. 3 (2021): 280–95.

75. Megan Gibson, "The Provocative History of French Weekly Newspaper Charlie Hebdo," *Time*, January 7, 2015.

76. Emily Greenhouse, "The Charlie Hebdo Affair: Laughing at Blasphemy," *The New Yorker*, September 28, 2012.

77. Brian Love, "France Bans Muhammad Cartoon Protests," *Christian Science Monitor*, September 21, 2012.

78. "Charlie Hebdo Row: Cartoons Divide French Press," BBC.com, September 20, 2012.

79. Don Murray, "France Even More Fractured after the Charlie Hebdo Rampage," CBCNews.com, January 8, 2015.

80. "A Muslim-Run France? Novel Sparks Islamophobia Row," France24.com, January 7, 2015.

81. "French, World Leaders Condemn Attack at Charlie Hebdo," France24.com, January 7, 2015.

82. "Charlie Hebdo Attack: Three Days of Terror," BBC.com, January 14, 2015.

83. Henry Samuel, "French Police Chief Committed Suicide after Charlie Hebdo Attack," *Telegraph*, January 12, 2015.

84. "French, World Leaders Condemn Attack at Charlie Hebdo," France24.

85. Myriam Francois, "France's Treatment of Its Muslim Citizens Is the True Measure of Its Republican Values," *Time*, December 8, 2020.

86. Charles Bremner, "Le Pen Fights Back with Religious Dress Ban," *Times* (UK), October 17, 2016.

87. Pierre Rimbert, "After the Paris Killings: Are You Charlie or Not?" *Le Monde Diplomatique* (Paris), February 5, 2015.

88. Christopher Caldwell, "Immigration and Islam: Europe's Crisis of Faith," *Wall Street Journal*, January 16, 2015.

89. Norimitsu Onishi, "Charlie Hebdo Republishes Cartoons That Prompted Deadly 2015 Attack," *New York Times*, September 1, 2020.

90. Constant Méheut, "Paris Suspect Said Attack Was Aimed at Paper That Mocked Islam's Prophet," *New York Times*, September 26, 2020.

91. Mustafa Akyol, "Yes, Islam Is Facing a Crisis. No, France Isn't Helping Solve It," Foreign Policy, November 20, 2020.

92. Carolyn Reid, "Macron's Crackdown on Islamist Separatism," *Towson University Journal of International Affairs* LIV, no. 2, (Spring 2021): 37–45.

Chapter Two

Freedom of Expression and Its Limitations in Europe

HISTORICAL OVERVIEW

We can trace the roots of freedom of expression in the idea of "liberty" as it transformed itself over a long period of time, especially in Europe. Liberty was the core concept from where different derivations of the word "freedom" got developed. We can say this on the basis of word etymology as the word "liberty" is derived from the Latin word *liber* meaning "free" that transformed into *libertas* and then Old French word *liberte* before becoming "liberty" in English,[1] while the word "freedom" evolved from the Old English word of *frēodōm*.[2] Europe saw a long period of the development of these concepts both being used interchangeably.[3] [4]

It is believed that during the sixth century BC in Athenian democracy, the concept of free speech developed.[5] The words *isegoria* and *parrhesia* were being used in ancient Greece, meaning "Freedom of Speech" but with a slight difference.[6] One of the ideas of such kind can also be seen in a speech delivered by Socrates in 399 BC before his prosecutors in which he openly defended the right to free speech: If you offered to let me off this time on condition, I am not any longer to speak my mind . . . I should say to you, "Men of Athens, I shall obey the Gods rather than you."

Socrates is considered to be the first voice to openly differ from prevalent norms and regulations of that time due to which he was persecuted. Persecution of Socrates gave the world an idea to think differently and honor the voices that differ from mainstream thought processes.[7] Freedom of speech can also be traced in Republican Rome as one of the core values.[8] One example appeared in a book titled *Meditations* by Roman emperor Marcus Aurelius (121–180 AD) in which he gave "idea of a polity in which there is the same law for all, a polity administered with regard to equal rights and equal freedom of speech, and the idea of a kingly government which respects most of all the freedom of the governed."[9]

However, the first cornerstone of liberty and civil rights in Europe was the Magna Carta signed in England on June 15, 1215. For the first time it documented that no one, including the king and the lawmakers, is above the law and everyone shall be given respective rights according to the law. The Magna Carta laid the foundation of the future institutionalization of freedom throughout the continent.

In 1516, during the period of the Renaissance, Dutch humanist and Catholic theologian Erasmus wrote his famous book titled *The Education of a Christian Prince* in which he wrote: "In a free state, tongues too should be free."[10] Passed on June 7, 1628, in England, the Petition of Right gave particular liberties to the subjects including the assurance that disagreeing with the government cannot become basis for anyone's arrest. The first formal usage of the term "free speech" is seen in the *Institutes of the Laws of England (1628–44)* by Sir Edward Coke.[11]

In 1633, Italian astronomer Galileo Galilei (1564–1642) was put under house arrest for stating that the earth revolves around the sun contrary to the then Christian belief. However, this was done by force at that time and a wave of awakening had already started among the educated people regarding freedom to express one's belief and scientific findings. An English man of letters, John Milton (1608–1674) published a pamphlet in 1644 criticizing parliamentary legislation to put censorship on press and publications. His pamphlet titled *Areopagitica* was a milestone in the generation of thinking against state controlled publication and freedom of press. He wrote, "None can love freedom heartily, but good men; the rest love not freedom, but license."[12] Milton described that the right to freedom of speech is not confined to express one's thoughts through any means but it has three distinct features: the right to *seek*, *receive*, and *impart* information and ideas.

In 1689, the England's Parliament passed the Bill of Rights that ensured certain basic civil rights and liberties. It granted "freedom of speech in the parliament" as the members were allowed to speak freely after this legislation.[13]

Although this freedom to speak freely was granted only to the elected members, it was the first state-level recognition of this right that paved the way for future legislations. French philosopher and enlightenment writer Voltaire (1694–1778) was a blunt advocate of freedom of speech. His well-known letter to Abbot le Riche, written in 1770, represents his thoughts on freedom of speech. He wrote, "I detest what you write, but I would give my life to make it possible for you to continue to write."[14]

The French Revolution helped Europe evolve and formulate fundamental principles of freedom and liberty. This period was instrumental in developing the European school of thought on *liberty*, *equality*, and *fraternity*. The

French Revolution not only gave political and intellectual connotations to the concept of freedom, it also provided some legal and constitutional basis to it. In 1789, The Declaration of the Rights of Man and the Citizen was passed during the French Revolution that gave legal cover with prime importance to the right of free speech.[15]

The First Amendment to the United States Constitution adopted in 1791 was instrumental in spreading and legitimizing the idea of free speech not only in the United States but also the whole world. English philosopher John Stuart Mill (1806–1873) chalked out fundamental principles for the freedom of expression through his writings. His theory of liberty, explained in a philosophical essay titled *On Liberty* written in 1859, is considered highly influential in shaping ideas of social and political freedom. Mill writes, "Unmeasured vituperation, employed on the side of prevailing opinion, really does deter people from expressing contrary opinions, and from listening to those who express them."[16]

Although the right to express oneself was protected to an extent in some legislation across Europe and the United States, by the twentieth century institutionalization of human rights as a whole was started on a global level. Firstly, more focus was on humanitarian laws, but with the passage of two world wars the need to have a comprehensive body of human rights legislation was felt with gravity.

RELEVANT LAWS

Freedom of expression in today's world is recognized in international and regional human rights laws. The first milestone legislation in this regard on a global level was inclusion of this right in the Universal Declaration of Human Rights adopted on December 10, 1948. Article 19 of the Declaration guarantees the right to freedom of opinion and expression.[17] Article 19 of the International Covenant on Civil and Political Rights (ICCPR)[18] adopted by the General Assembly of the United Nations on December 19, 1966, also enshrines this right in explicit words. In addition to the Universal Declaration of Human Rights, different world regions adopted different bodies of laws to ensure freedom of expression. Article 13 of the American Convention on Human Rights and Article 9 of the African Charter on Human and Peoples' Rights guarantee this right. Right to freedom of expression is also protected in Article 15(3)[19] of The International Covenant on Economic, Social and Cultural Rights.

In exclusive European context, institutionalization of the freedom of expression can be traced back to The Declaration of the Rights of the Man and of the Citizen[20] set by France's National Constituent Assembly in 1789 during the French Revolution.[21] Freedom of expression, subject to certain restrictions, is mandated in Article 10[22] of the European Convention on Human Rights ECHR. The Charter of Fundamental Rights of the European Union[23] ratified on December 7, 2000, also talks about freedom of expression in Article 11.

EU Human Rights Guidelines on Freedom of Expression Online and Offline were passed by the Council of the European Union on May 12, 2014.[24] These guidelines set priorities for the European Union in terms of freedom of expression in its partner countries all over the globe.[25]

Among European states, *Grundloven* (The Constitutional Act of Denmark 1953) secures the right to freely write, speak, and publish any idea[26] without any censorship. The French Constitution of 1958 incorporates Article 11 of the Declaration of the Rights of Man of 1789 to protect freedom of expression as an "essential freedom." Conseil supérieur de l'audiovisuel (Superior Council on Audiovisual) regulates under the relevant French laws whatever is broadcast. The Federal Constitution of 1949 (or Basic Law) of Germany gives protection to the freedom of expression[27] under Article 5. The Constitution of the Kingdom of the Netherlands lays down in detail rights of the citizens to openly express their thoughts[28] without any prior approval. In the United Kingdom, there is no specific legal instrument to protect freedom of expression, however, the Human Rights Act of 1998 refers to the duties of the state to act under ECHR in terms of granting the right to freedom of expression to its citizens.[29]

CONTEMPORARY DEFINITIONS AND DEBATES

The concept of freedom of expression always coincides with that of hate speech. The biggest questions that remains are what the limits of freedom of expression are, what are its kinds, and from where hate speech begins. This debate is lasting since the concept of freedom of expression prevails, and after 9/11 it transformed into a heated debate all around the world and especially in Europe. Like other terminologies frequently used in social sciences (e.g., "terrorism"), both freedom of expression and hate speech lack comprehensive and agreed-upon definitions. UNGA, in its meeting in January 1948, passed Resolution no. 59 favoring freedom of expression while providing one of the initial definitions of this concept in these words: "Freedom of information implies the right to gather, transmit and publish news anywhere and everywhere without fetters. As such it is an essential factor in any serious effort to promote the peace and progress of the world."[30]

In general, freedom of expression means to express one's thinking by any means without any restrictions, the Oxford Dictionary also suggests the same: "The power or right to express one's opinions without censorship, restraint, or legal penalty."[31] In Merriam-Webster freedom of speech has been described as more legal than social or political right and is described as "the legal right to express one's opinions freely."[32]

We also find definitions emphasizing a correlation between freedom of expression and democracy, such as, "Free speech and expression is the lifeblood of democracy, facilitating open debate, the proper consideration of diverse interests and perspectives."[33]

There are several debates centered on the concept of freedom of expression. Primarily, there is a general consensus that freedom of expression is a basic human right and it is directly linked to "individual liberty" and "self-fulfillment." It is also attributed to "freedom of choice" and "diversity" being core values of a liberal society.[34] Thinkers like John Stuart Mill regard freedom of expression vital to acquire knowledge and enhance it. Mill thinks that freedom of expression is a step forward in search of truth:

> The peculiar evil of silencing the expression of an opinion is, that it is robbing the human race; posterity as well as the existing generation; those who dissent from the opinion, still more than those who hold it. If the opinion is right, they are deprived of the opportunity of exchanging error for truth: if wrong, they lose, what is almost as great a benefit, the clearer perception and livelier impression of truth, produced by its collision with error.[35]

Some writers have distinguished between the *freedom of speech* and *freedom of expression* terming the latter more comprehensive but more complex at the same time.[36] Some like Stanley Fish have argued that there is nothing what we call free speech because there is no existence of literally any absolute and unlimited free speech.[37] Alan Hayworth also says that people do not exercise the right to express themselves as we assume that they have the right to do so by referring to the phrase "free speech."[38]

But in response to this, there is an argument that unpopular, unfair, and even untrue expressions should also be allowed and remedy to this "bad speech" is "more speech." This is a very popular notion in favor of unlimited free speech enshrined in some landmark US Supreme Court judgments. Justice Brandeis wrote, "If there be time to expose through discussion the falsehood and fallacies, to avert the evil by the processes of education, the remedy to be applied is more speech, not enforced silence.[39]

Another judgment proposes a "marketplace of ideas" derived from the First Amendment to the US Constitution. In his judgment, Justice Holmes favors a "free trade of ideas" so that the powerful idea can compete in the market of ideas: "The ultimate good desired is better reached by free trade in ideas—that the best test of truth is the power of the thought to get itself accepted in the competition of the market."[40]

THEORETICAL AND LEGAL LIMITATIONS

John Stuart Mill, in *On Liberty*, talked about limitations to the freedom of speech under the "harm principle" being "rightfully exercised" in order to "prevent harm to others" in these words: "The only purpose for which power can be rightfully exercised over any member of a civilized community, against his will, is to prevent harm to others."[41] In response to the "harm principle," Joel Feinberg talked about the "offense principle" while differentiating between "harmful" and "offensive." His words are:

> It is always a good reason in support of a proposed criminal prohibition that it would probably be an effective way of preventing serious offense . . . to persons other than the actor, and that it is probably a necessary means to that end. . . . The principle asserts, in effect, that the prevention of offensive conduct is properly the state's business.[42]

But Feinberg's offense principle has also been criticized by thinkers as there can be many forms and manifestations of offense and it will be difficult to ascertain what act should be called an offense and vice versa.[43] The *Stanford Encyclopedia of Philosophy* writes that the freedom of speech has to be limited and every society, according to its own norms and values, would decide what to protect as a right to freedom of speech and what not.[44]

The International Covenant on Civil and Political Rights talks about certain limitations to the freedom of speech in Article 19(3) and in Article 20[45] as it talks about prohibition of the "propaganda for war" and any sort of "hatred" or "incitement." The International Convention on the Elimination of Racial Discrimination (ICERD)[46] also incorporates certain restrictions on the freedom of expression with much broader spectrum to be applied by signatory states. But both ICCPR and ICERD appear to be inconsistent when read together in terms of imposing restrictions on certain types of expression. Collectively, they fail to provide a clear, legal guideline to member states on how to limit freedom of speech.

In Europe, Article 52(1)[47] of the Charter of Fundamental Rights of the European Union places some restrictions on the freedom of expression. Also, Additional Protocol to the Convention on Cybercrime, Concerning the Criminalisation of Acts of a Racist and Xenophobic Nature Committed through Computer Systems[48] was signed on November 7, 2002, and deals with some aspects of hate speech. It criminalizes usage of computer systems to proliferate racist and xenophobic material.

ECHR does not bar any member state from restricting freedom of expression and only provides three steps to examine the legitimacy of any state intervention. But the European Court of Human Rights has given rulings in which it placed limitations on certain expressions. On October 25, 2018, ECtHR unanimously dismissed the appeal of an Austrian woman against domestic court judgments.

The woman was convicted by domestic courts for insulting the Prophet Muhammad. The convict approached the ECtHR pleading that Article 10 of the European Convention on Human Rights gives her the right of freedom of expression. But the ECtHR upheld the domestic court judgments by saying that she was rightly convicted.[49] In this case, ECtHR evaluated whether limiting the right to freedom of expression was "prescribed by law," had a "legitimate aim" and was "necessary in a democratic society."[50] The court said that the Austrian courts "carefully balanced" the freedom of expression and religion[51] and ruled that it is not permissible to hurt anyone's feelings[52] by misinterpreting Article 10 of the European Convention on Human Rights.

In major European countries, France limits the freedom of expression under the Law of July 29, 1881, on Freedom of the Press along with the 1789 Declaration. This law with several amendments over the time defines "defamation" and "insult" as well. Furthermore, there is a limit to speak against institutions and officeholders and inciting criminal acts is also prohibited by law.[53] Germany gives top priority to the right to dignity and personal honor. Article 1 of the Basic Law of Germany talks about the inviolability of the human dignity[54] while Article 5 states that all rights including freedom of expression shall be limited when the question of "personal honor" arises.[55] Article 18[56] also limits freedom of expression when it endangers the "free democratic basic order." In the United Kingdom, Public Order Act 1986 Part III deals at length with hatred on the basis of race, religion, and sexual orientation.

BLASPHEMY LAWS AND SOVEREIGN IMMUNITIES

Few states in Europe still exercise principle of lèse-majesté, a Latin phrase securing dignity of the sovereign (literal meaning: injured majesty)[57] and blasphemy laws are still in force in some states as well. Austria has a clause related to blasphemy in its criminal code[58] and the woman E. S. was convicted under the same law by domestic court. The constitution in Belgium clearly mentions inviolability of the king[59] in Article 88. Danish constitution also declares the king "sacrosanct" who cannot be held accountable in person,[60] however, according to Article 63, courts can decide cases related to executive authority. In 2017, Denmark abolished a very old blasphemy law and in the same year a man was charged under this law for burning the Qur'an and streaming it on Facebook.[61] Finland has a blasphemy law[62] and on June 8, 2012, Jussi Halla-aho, a Finnish member of Parliament, was convicted by the Supreme Court of Finland for hate speech against Muslims and immigrants.[63]

Halla-aho later became the leader of the Finns Party and a member of the European Parliament representing Finland. France does not have any blasphemy law. Articles 24 and 32 of the 1881 law on the freedom of the press are invoked against religious insult but without much success.[64] German criminal law penalizes for insulting religion[65] and a man was convicted under the same law for insulting Islam in 2006 when he was offering toilet paper to mosques having "Koran" written on them.[66] In Iceland, whoever exercises presidential authority is not answerable for their official acts.[67] No criminal proceeding can begin against the president without parliamentary approval according to the constitution of the republic. The Irish case is interesting in the sense that it enacted a blasphemy law in 2009 and the then government favored framing a blasphemy law as the country's constitution protected only Christians for their belief. Under the same law, a complaint was lodged in 2017 against English actor Stephen Fry for insulting God, but the case was immediately closed by the police[68] and the law was ultimately repealed in January 2020 amid severe criticism.[69] Before that, the film *Monty Python's Life of Brian* was also banned in 1979 by censorship authority for being blasphemous.[70] The Italian constitution[71] also gives immunity to the president; they can only be impeached by Parliament if they commit high treason or subverts the constitution. Also, damaging "honor or prestige" of the president[72] is punishable with imprisonment of one to five years and committing blasphemy is also a crime under articles 403 and 404[73] of the criminal code. Norway also gives immunity to its king through its constitution,[74] but abolished blasphemy law in 2009. The last action taken under the defunct blasphemy law was banning the British comedy film *Monty Python's Life of Brian* in 1980. The film was briefly banned for insulting Jesus.[75] Although Poland does not have any blasphemy laws, criminal code[76] has been used to convict people for this crime. In recent years, pop star Doda was fined for insulting the Bible in 2012[77] and before that, in 2005, renowned journalist Jerzy Urban was found guilty of "mocking the Pope."[78] The Spanish monarch also enjoys inviolability[79] under the national constitution, and its criminal code[80] also penalizes for blasphemy and hatred. Famous artist Javier Krahe was prosecuted but then acquitted in 2012 for blasphemy[81] and actor Willy Toledo was also charged with blasphemy and acquitted in 2020.[82] Sweden provides its emperor[83] with constitutional immunity through its constitution and also has a law that protects religious and other minority groups from discrimination. The said law has primarily been used by Jews and homosexuals. Swiss penal code, through its Article 261 (Attack on the freedom of faith and the freedom to worship),[84] guarantees the freedom to worship. In the United Kingdom, the Crown Proceedings Act 1947 governs immunity to the Crown in many respects. The Crown in person is immune from all civil and criminal proceedings and can only be tried when permitted by the Crown Proceedings Act while performing as the government. Blasphemy law in the United Kingdom was never approved by Parliament rather blasphemy was declared a crime by nineteenth-century judges in order to protect the Church of England. This was one of the main reasons of criticism, too, as other beliefs were not protected and in 2008 Parliament abolished the relevant common law.[85] *Visions of Ecstasy* was the only film banned in 1989 for being blasphemous and the same was cleared in 2012.[86] Northern Ireland and Scotland still have dormant blasphemy laws and there are active campaigns to abolish them.[87]

Figure 2.1. European countries having blasphemy legislation (2018).

Source: https://www.france24.com/en/20181031-blasphemy-middle-east-asia-bibi-europe-law-religion-ireland

HATE SPEECH AND HOLOCAUST DENIAL LAWS

While Articles 19 and 20 of ICCPR talk about limiting hate speech on a global level, there is no particular legal instrument in Europe to stop hate speech. However, the Council Framework Decision of November 28, 2008, on Combating Certain Forms and Expressions of Racism and Xenophobia by Means of Criminal Law came into force on December 6, 2008, and asks member states to stop racism and xenophobia in their multiple forms. This decision also mentions hate speech and its limitations[88] and criminalizes the offenses concerning racism and xenophobia. It focuses on the Nuremberg trials against Nazis and prohibits their denial, condoning, and trivializing.[89] However, this Framework is not binding on member states but still has inspiring status.

Additionally, the Protocol to the Convention on Cybercrime[90] prohibits approving, justifying, denying, or grossly minimizing genocide and crimes against humanity particularly the Holocaust. When the European Union adopted laws to criminalize denial of the Holocaust, Muslims objected by saying that the EU did not legislate on hate crimes against Muslims. Also, during this legislation Baltic States wanted mentioning of atrocities done by Stalin but that was denied too.[91] In October 2019, the European Court of Human Rights declared[92] that Holocaust denial is not protected by European Convention on Human Rights.[93]

At the state level in Europe, Austria has the most strict laws against Holocaust denial. Its National Socialism Prohibition Act 1947[94] has several clauses dealing with denial and criminalization of the Holocaust. According to the same laws, noted British historian David Irving was sentenced to three years in prison for denying the Holocaust.[95] The Belgian Centre for Equal Opportunities and Opposition to Racism (CEOOR) prosecutes under the law of March 23, 1995,[96] against anyone who denies or grossly minimizes the Holocaust.[97]

In the Czech Republic, the Law against Support and Dissemination of Movements Oppressing Human Rights and Freedoms of 2001[98] deals with the offense of creating doubts or publicly negating Nazi genocide.[99] Danish penal code[100] has a strong clause to prevent hate speech and includes multiple factors.[101] French law prohibits hate speech and denial of crimes against humanity with a special focus on the Holocaust[102] suggesting a penalty of up to a year in prison and a fine of 45,000 euros.[103]

Criminal code in Germany deals with both hate speech[104] and Holocaust denial[105] and has punishments from three months to five years. Greek law[106] criminalizes the approval and denial of the Holocaust with penalties. In 2010, the Hungarian parliament again passed a law against denial of the Holocaust[107] after the country's top constitutional court repealed it in 1992.[108] Italy amended its law of 1975 in 2016 including denial of the Holocaust[109] into the list of crimes[110] and also forbids hate speech under Article 405[111] of the criminal code.

Liechtenstein, one of the smallest countries in Europe, also bars people from denying or justifying genocide and crimes against humanity.[112] However, its law does not mention the Holocaust in particular.[113] In the Baltic states, the criminal code of Lithuania penalizes[114] for denying or approving the Nazi and USSR crimes.[115] Luxembourg also outlaws denial of the Holocaust[116] and other genocides.[117] Also, the criminal code in the Netherlands prohibits insult of anyone on the basis of race, religion, or other preferences and the same law[118] has been used to penalize Holocaust denial.[119]

Poland is unique in the sense that it established an Institute of National Remembrance – Commission for the Prosecution of Crimes against the Polish Nation *(Instytut Pamięci Narodowej – Komisja Ścigania Zbrodni przeciwko Narodowi Polskiemu)* and an act[120] establishing this institute also governs the law against denial of Nazi and Communist atrocities.[121] It also criminalizes hate speech[122] under the criminal code. Portugal does not have any Holocaust-specific laws, but Article 240 of the criminal code prohibits racial, religious, or sexual discrimination and denial of war crimes and crimes against peace and humanity.[123]

Romania promulgated an Emergency Ordinance[124] in 2002 to criminalize hate speech and Holocaust denial. Penal law in Slovakia also declares it a crime[125] to deny the Holocaust. Holocaust denial was a crime in Spain until 2007 when the Constitutional Court declared it unconstitutional.[126] Switzerland has not criminalized Holocaust denial but its criminal code[127] mentions similar crimes in general.

The United Kingdom does not have any Holocaust denial law but prohibits hate speech and hate crimes by several acts including the Public Order Act 1986, the Criminal Justice and Public Order Act 1994, the Crime and Disorder Act 1998, the Racial and Religious Hatred Act 2006, and the Criminal Justice and Immigration Act 2008. Sometimes, these laws are criticized for being harsh and their usage being discriminatory. On March 15, 2012, a young Muslim boy named Azhar Ahmed was charged with treason for making comments on Facebook against UK military involvement in Afghanistan. On this, *The Guardian* called the United Kingdom a "total policing state" that 'racialized' this issue by giving absolute superiority to white people.[128] *The Independent* termed it "terrifying new censorship" with a "debased and demoralized view of freedom."[129]

NOTES

1. *Lexico–powered by Oxford*, s.v. "Liberty."

2. Ibid.

3. *Stanford Encyclopedia of Philosophy*, s.v. "Positive and Negative Liberty."

4. Hanna Fenichel Pitkin, "Are Freedom and Liberty Twins?" *Political Theory* 16, no. 4 (November 1988): 523–52.

5. Kurt Raaflaub, Josiah Ober, and Robert Wallace, *Origins of Democracy in Ancient Greece* (Berkeley: University of California Press, 2007), 65.

6. Teresa M. Bejan, "The Two Clashing Meanings of Free Speech," *The Atlantic*, December 2, 2017.

7. Zechariah Chafee Jr., *Freedom's Prophet: Selected Writings of Zechariah Chafee*, ed., Edward Domenic Re (New York: Oceana Publications, 1981), 162.

8. M. P. Charlesworth, "Freedom of Speech in Republican Rome," *The Classical Review* 57, no. 1 (March 1943): 49.

9. Marcus Aurelius, *Meditations*, trans. Robin Hard (Hertfordshire: Wordsworth Editions Limited, 1997), 170.

10. Desiderius Erasmus, *Erasmus: The Education of a Christian Prince with the Panegyric for Archduke Philip of Austria*, ed. Lisa Jardine (Cambridge: Cambridge University Press, 1997), 88.

11. Edward Coke, *The Third Part of the Institutes of the Laws of England: Concerning High Treason, and Other Pleas of the Crown, and Criminall Causes* (London: M. Flesher for W. Lee, and D. Pakeman, 1644), 8–9.

12. Rufus Wilmot Griswold, ed., *The Prose Works of John Milton* (Philadelphia: H. Hooker, 1845), 374.

13. Article 9 reads: "Freedome of Speech and Debates or Proceedings in Parlyament ought not to be impeached or questioned in any Court or Place out of Parlyament."

14. Michael Haas, *International Human Rights: A Comprehensive Introduction* (New York: Routledge, 2014), 28.

15. Article 11 reads: "The free communication of ideas and opinions is one of the most precious of the rights of man. Every citizen may, accordingly, speak, write, and print with freedom, but shall be responsible for such abuses of this freedom as shall be defined by law."

16. John Stuart Mill, *On Liberty*, Harvard Classics (New York: PF Collier & Sons Company, 1909), 25:258.

17. It reads: "Everyone has the right to freedom of opinion and expression; this right includes freedom to hold opinions without interference and to seek, receive and impart information and ideas through any media and regardless of frontiers."

18. Article 19 of the Covenant reads: "1. Everyone shall have the right to hold opinions without interference. 2. Everyone shall have the right to freedom of expression; this right shall include freedom to seek, receive and impart information and ideas of all kinds, regardless of frontiers, either orally, in writing or in print, in the form of art, or through any other media of his choice. 3. The exercise of the rights provided for in paragraph 2 of this article carries with it special duties and responsi-

bilities. It may therefore be subject to certain restrictions, but these shall only be such as are provided by law and are necessary: (a) For respect of the rights or reputations of others; (b) For the protection of national security or of public order (ordre public), or of public health or morals."

19. It reads: "The States Parties to the present Covenant undertake to respect the freedom indispensable for scientific research and creative activity."

20. Article XI reads: "The free communication of thoughts and of opinions is one of the most precious rights of man: any citizen thus may speak, write, and print freely, except to respond to the abuse of this liberty, in the cases determined by the law."

21. Lynn Hunt, "The Declaration of the Rights of Man and of the Citizen, August 1789: A Revolutionary Document," in *Revolutionary Moments: Reading Revolutionary Texts*, ed. Rachel Hammersley (London: Bloomsbury Academic, 2015), 77–84.

22. "1. Everyone has the right to freedom of expression. This right shall include freedom to hold opinions and to receive and impart information and ideas without interference by public authority and regardless of frontiers. This Article shall not prevent States from requiring the licensing of broadcasting, television or cinema enterprises. 2. The exercise of these freedoms, since it carries with it duties and responsibilities, may be subject to such formalities, conditions, restrictions or penalties as are prescribed by law and are necessary in a democratic society, in the interests of national security, territorial integrity or public safety, for the prevention of disorder or crime, for the protection of health or morals, for the protection of the reputation or rights of others, for preventing the disclosure of information received in confidence, or for maintaining the authority and impartiality of the judiciary."

23. Article 11 reads: "1. Everyone has the right to freedom of expression. This right shall include freedom to hold opinions and to receive and impart information and ideas without interference by public authority and regardless of frontiers. 2. The freedom and pluralism of the media shall be respected."

24. It reads: "1. Combating violence, persecution, harassment and intimidation of individuals, including journalists and other media actors, because of their exercise of the right to freedom of expression online and offline, and combating impunity for such crimes. 2. Promoting laws and practices that protect freedom of opinion and expression. 3. Promoting media freedom and pluralism and fostering an understanding among public authorities of the dangers of unwarranted interference with impartial/critical reporting. 4. Promoting and respecting human rights in cyberspace and other information and communication technologies. 5. Promoting best practices by companies. 6. Promoting legal amendments and practices aimed at strengthening data protection and privacy online/offline."

25. *EU Guidelines on Freedom of Expression Online and Offline 2014* (The Council of the European Union, 2014), 7–11.

26. Article 77 reads: "Any person shall be at liberty to publish his ideas in print, in writing, and in speech, subject to his being held responsible in a court of law. Censorship and other preventive measures shall never again be introduced."

27. Clause 1 of Article 5 reads: "Every person shall have the right freely to express and disseminate his opinions in speech, writing and pictures, and to inform himself without hindrance from generally accessible sources. Freedom of the press and free-

dom of reporting by means of broadcasts and films shall be guaranteed. There shall be no censorship."

28. Article 7 reads: "1. No one shall require prior permission to publish thoughts or opinions through the press, without prejudice to the responsibility of every person under the law. 2. Rules concerning radio and television shall be laid down by Act of Parliament. There shall be no prior supervision of the content of a radio or television broadcast. 3. No one shall be required to submit thoughts or opinions for prior approval in order to disseminate them by means other than those mentioned in the preceding paragraphs, without prejudice to the responsibility of every person under the law. The holding of performances open to persons younger than sixteen years of age may be regulated by Act of Parliament in order to protect good morals."

29. Brittan Heller and Joris van Hoboken, *Freedom of Expression: A Comparative Summary of United States and European Law* (Amsterdam: Transatlantic Working Group, 2019), 12.

30. Ibid., 14–15.

31. *Lexico–powered by Oxford*, s.v. "Freedom of Speech."

32. *Merriam-Webster Dictionary*, s.v. "Freedom of Speech."

33. *Freedom House*, s.v. "Freedom of Expression."

34. Heller and Hoboken, *Freedom of Expression*, 2.

35 Mill, *On Liberty*, 35.

36. Paul Finkelman, ed., *Encyclopedia of American Civil Liberties* (New York: Routledge, 2006), s.v. "Philosophy and Theory of Freedom of Expression."

37. Stanley Fish, *There's No Such Thing as Free Speech . . . and It's a Good Thing Too* (New York: Oxford University Press, 1994), 100–2.

38. Alan Hayworth, *Free Speech* (New York: Routledge, 2002), 11.

39. Louis Brandeis, "Whitney v. California [1927]," Cornell Law School, May 16, 1927.

40. Oliver Wendell Holmes, "Abrams v. United States," Cornell Law School, November 10, 1919.

41. Mill, *On Liberty*, 23.

42. Joel Feinberg, *Offense to Others: The Moral Limits of the Criminal Law* (Oxford: Oxford University Press, 1985), 1.

43. Jasper Doomen, "Freedom and Equality as Necessary Constituents of a Liberal Democratic State" (diss., Department of Encyclopedia and Philosophy of Law, Faculty of Law, Leiden University, 2014), 100–1.

44. *Stanford Encyclopedia of Philosophy*, s.v. "Freedom of Speech."

45. Article 20 of the Covenant reads: "1. Any propaganda for war shall be prohibited by law. 2. Any advocacy of national, racial or religious hatred that constitutes incitement to discrimination, hostility or violence shall be prohibited by law."

46. Article 4(a) requires States to "condemn all propaganda and all organizations which are based on ideas or theories of superiority of one race or group of persons of one colour or ethnic origin, or which attempt to justify or promote racial hatred and discrimination in any form."

47. Article 52(1) reads: "Any limitation on the exercise of the rights and freedoms ecognized by this Charter must be provided for by law and respect the essence of

those rights and freedoms. Subject to the principle of proportionality, limitations may be made only if they are necessary and genuinely meet objectives of general interest ecognized by the Union or the need to protect the rights and freedoms of others."

48. Article 3 of Chapter II reads: "Each Party shall adopt such legislative and other measures as may be necessary to establish as criminal offences under its domestic law, when committed intentionally and without right, the following conduct: distributing, or otherwise making available, racist and xenophobic material to the public through a computer system."

49. Para 58 reads: "Court considers that the domestic courts did not overstep their – wide – margin of appreciation in the instant case when convicting the applicant of disparaging religious doctrines. Accordingly, there has been no violation of Article 10 of the Convention."

50. "E. S. vs Austria," European Court of Human Rights, October 25, 2018.

51. Para 57 reads: "The domestic courts comprehensively assessed the wider context of the applicant's statements, and carefully balanced her right to freedom of expression with the rights of others to have their religious feelings protected and to have religious peace preserved in Austrian society. They discussed the permissible limits of criticism of religious doctrines versus their disparagement, and found that the applicant's statements had been likely to arouse justified indignation in Muslims. In addition, the Court considers that the impugned statements were not phrased in a neutral manner aimed at making an objective contribution to a public debate concerning child marriages . . ., but amounted to a generalisation without a factual basis. Thus, by considering them as going beyond the permissible limits of an objective debate and classifying them as an abusive attack on the Prophet of Islam, which was capable of stirring up prejudice and putting religious peace at risk, the domestic courts came to the conclusion that the facts at issue contained elements of incitement to religious intolerance."

52. Para 55 reads: "As to the applicant's argument that a few individual statements had to be tolerated during a lively discussion, the Court considers that it is not compatible with Article 10 of the Convention to package incriminating statements in the wrapping of an otherwise acceptable expression of opinion and deduce that this renders statements exceeding the permissible limits of freedom of expression passable. Moreover, the applicant was wrong to assume that improper attacks on religious groups had to be tolerated even if they were based on untrue facts. On the contrary, the Court has held that statements which are based on (manifestly) untrue facts do not enjoy the protection of Article 10."

53. "Limits On Freedom of Expression: France," Library of Congress.

54. Clause 1 of Article 1 reads: "Human dignity shall be inviolable. To respect and protect it shall be the duty of all state authority."

55. Clause 2 of Article 5 reads: "[Freedom of expression rights] shall find their limits in the provisions of general laws, in provisions for the protection of young persons, and in the right to personal honor."

56. Article 18 reads: "Whoever abuses the freedom of expression . . . in order to combat the free democratic basic order shall forfeit these basic rights. This forfeiture and its extent shall be declared by the Federal Constitutional Court."

57. *Merriam-Webster Dictionary*, s.v. "Lèse-Majesté."

58. Clause 188 in the eighth section reads: "Anyone who publicly degrades or ridicules a person or a thing that is the subject of veneration of a church or religious society existing in the country, or a doctrine, a legally permissible custom or a legally permissible institution of such a church or religious society, under which his conduct is capable of causing justified annoyance, is punished with imprisonment of up to six months or with a fine of up to 360 daily rates."

59. Article 88 reads: *"The King's person is inviolable; his ministers are accountable."*

60. Article 13 reads: "The King cannot be charged for his acts; his person is sacrosanct. Ministers are responsible for government leadership; their accountability is determined by law" (unofficial translation).

61. Kimiko de Freytas-Tamura, "Danish Man Who Burned Quran Is Prosecuted for Blasphemy," *New York Times*, February 23, 2017.

62. Section 10 of the criminal code reads: "A person who: (1) publicly blasphemes against God or, for the purpose of offending, publicly defames or desecrates what is otherwise held to be sacred by a church or religious community, as referred to in the Act on the Freedom of Religion, or (2) by making noise, acting threateningly or otherwise, disturbs worship, ecclesiastical proceedings, other similar religious proceedings or a funeral, shall be sentenced for a breach of the sanctity of religion to a fine or to imprisonment for at most six months" (unofficial translation).

63. Jeroen Temperman and András Koltay, eds., *Blasphemy and Freedom of Expression: Comparative, Theoretical and Historical Reflections after the Charlie Hebdo Massacre* (Cambridge: Cambridge University Press, 2017), 331.

64. "Violating Rights: Enforcing the World's Blasphemy Laws," (Washington, DC: United States Commission on International Religious Freedom, 2020), 7.

65. Section 166 reads: "(1) Whoever publicly or by disseminating material (section 11 (3)) reviles the religion or ideology of others in a manner which is suitable for causing a disturbance of the public peace incurs a penalty of imprisonment for a term not exceeding three years or a fine. (2) Whoever publicly or by disseminating material (section 11 (3)) reviles a church or other religious or ideological community in Germany or its institutions or customs in a manner which is suitable for causing a disturbance of the public peace incurs the same penalty."

66. Bernan Assoc, *Parliamentary Assembly, Working Papers: 2007 Ordinary Session (Third Part),* (Strasbourg: Council of Europe Publishing, 2007), 215.

67. Article 11 reads: "The President of the Republic may not be held accountable for executive acts. The same applies to those who exercise presidential authority. The President may not be prosecuted on a criminal charge except with the consent of Althingi."

68. Henry McDonald, "Irish Police Halt Investigation of Stephen Fry for Blasphemy," *Guardian*, May 9, 2017.

69. Lawrence Cuny, *Freedom & Creativity: Defending Art, Defending Diversity (Special Edition)* (Paris: UNESCO, 2020), 14.

70. "An Awful Dump: The Ireland That Banned Monty Python's Life of Brian," *Irish Times*, February 26, 2019.

71. Article 90 reads: "The President of the Republic is not responsible for the actions performed in the exercise of the presidential duties, except in the case of high treason or attempt against the Constitution. In such cases, the President may be impeached by Parliament in joint session, with an absolute majority of its members."

72. Article 278 of the penal code reads: "Anyone who offends the honor or prestige of the President of the Republic is punished with imprisonment of one to five years."

73. Article 403 reads: "Anyone who publicly offends a religious confession, through the vilification of those who profess it, is punished with a fine from € 1,000 to € 5,000. A fine of € 2,000 to € 6,000 is applied to those who offend a religious confession, through the vilification of a minister of worship." Article 404 reads: "Anyone, in a place intended for worship, or in a public place or open to the public, offending a religious confession, vilifies with insulting expressions things that form the object of worship, or are consecrated to worship, or are necessarily intended for the exercise of worship, or commits the fact on the occasion of religious services, performed in a private place by a minister of worship, is punished with a fine from € 1,000 to € 5,000. Anyone who publicly and intentionally destroys, disperses, deteriorates, renders or dirties things that form an object of worship or are consecrated to worship or are necessarily destined for the exercise of worship is punished with imprisonment of up to two years."

74. Article 5 reads: "The King's person cannot be censured or accused. The responsibility rests with his Council."

75. Douglas McCall, Monty Python: A Chronology, 1969–2012 (Jefferson, NC: McFarland and Company, 2014), 74.

76. Article 196 reads: "Whoever insults the religious feelings of other people, profaning the subject of public religious worship or a place intended for public performance of religious rites, the penalty of restriction of liberty or imprisonment of up to 2 years."

77. Scott Maniquet, "Polish Pop Singer Found Guilty of Insulting Bible," *National Post (Toronto)*, January 19, 2012.

78. Kamil Tchorek, "Polish Court Fines Satirist for Mocking Name of the Pope," *Independent*, January 26, 2005.

79. Article 56(3) reads: "The person of the King is inviolable and is not subject to liability. Their acts will always be countersigned in the manner established in article 64, lacking validity without such endorsement, except as provided in article 65.2."

80. Article 525 of the Spanish Civil Code reads: "1. Those that, in order to offend the feelings of members of a religious confession, make public derision, orally, by writing or through any type of document, of their dogmas, beliefs, rituals or ceremonies or mistreat, also publicly, those who practice that religion, will be punished with a fine between eight to twelve month of their salary. 2. Those that make public derision, orally or by writing, of people who do not confess any religion will incur in the penalties set in the previous paragraph."

81. Juan Cruz, "Blasphemy ain't what it used to be," *El Pais English (Spain),* June 13, 2012.

82. "Madrid Court Acquits Spanish Actor of Blasphemy Complaint," *The Local (Spain)*, March 1, 2020.

83. Article 8 of Chapter 5 reads: "The King or Queen who is Head of State cannot be prosecuted for his or her actions. Nor can a Regent be prosecuted for his or her actions as Head of State.

84. Article 261 reads: "Any person who publicly and maliciously insults or mocks the religious convictions of others, and in particularly their belief in God, or maliciously desecrates objects of religious veneration, any person who maliciously prevents, disrupts or publicly mocks an act of worship, the conduct of which is guaranteed by the Constitution, or any person who maliciously desecrates a place or object that is intended for a religious ceremony or an act of worship the conduct of which is guaranteed by the Constitution, is liable to a monetary penalty."

85. Kim Murphy, "Britain's Blasphemy Law No Longer Sacred," *Los Angeles Times*, March 6, 2008.

86. Andrew Pulver, "Visions of Ecstasy Cleared for Release after 23 Years," *Guardian*, January 31, 2012.

87. "Religion and Free Speech: Blasphemy Laws Are Quietly Vanishing in Liberal Democracies," *The Economist*, August 25, 2019.

88. According to this decision: "Certain forms of conduct as outlined below, are punishable as criminal offences: 1. Public incitement to violence or hatred directed against a group of persons or a member of such a group defined on the basis of race, colour, descent, religion or belief, or national or ethnic origin; 2. The above-mentioned offence when carried out by the public dissemination or distribution of tracts, pictures or other material; 3. Publicly condoning, denying or grossly rivializing crimes of genocide, crimes against humanity and war crimes as defined in the Statute of the International Criminal Court (Articles 6, 7 and 8) and crimes defined in Article 6 of the Charter of the International Military Tribunal, when the conduct is carried out in a manner likely to incite violence or hatred against such a group or a member of such a group."

89. Clause (d) of Article 1 declares these crimes punishable: "Publicly condoning, denying or grossly rivializing the crimes defined in Article 6 of the Charter of the International Military Tribunal appended to the London Agreement of 8 August 1945, directed against a group of persons or a member of such a group defined by reference to race, colour, religion, descent or national or ethnic origin when the conduct is carried out in a manner likely to incite to violence or hatred against such a group or a member of such a group."

90. Article 6(1) reads: "Each Party shall adopt such legislative measures as may be necessary to establish the following conduct as criminal offences under its domestic law, when committed intentionally and without right: distributing or otherwise making available, through a computer system to the public, material which denies, grossly minimises, approves or justifies acts constituting genocide or crimes against humanity, as defined by international law and recognised as such by final and binding decisions of the International Military Tribunal, established by the London Agreement of 8 August 1945, or of any other international court established by relevant international instruments and whose jurisdiction is recognised by that Party."

91. Dan Bilefsky, "EU Adopts Measure Outlawing Holocaust Denial," *New York Times*, April 19, 2007.

92. Press release by ECtHR reads: "The case concerned the conviction of a Land deputy for denying the Holocaust during a speech in the regional Parliament. The Court found in particular that the applicant had intentionally stated untruths to defame Jews. Such statements could not attract the protection for freedom of speech offered by the Convention as they ran counter to the values of the Convention itself. There was thus no appearance of a violation of the applicant's rights and the complaint was inadmissible."

93. "Holocaust Denial is Not Protected by the European Convention on Human Rights," European Court of Human Rights media release, October 3, 2019.

94. Article 1, clause 3(h) reads: "In accordance with § 3g, anybody who denies, grossly minimizes, approves or seeks to justify the National Socialist genocide or any other National Socialist crimes against humanity in a publication, a broadcasting medium or any other medium publicly and in any other manner accessible to a large number of people will also be punished."

95. "David Irving Jailed for Holocaust Denial," *Guardian*, February 20, 2006.

96. Article 1 reads: "Whoever, in one of the circumstances indicated by Article 444 of the Penal Code, denies, grossly inimizes, tries to justify or approves of the genocide committed by the German National-Socialist regime during the Second World War will be punished by imprisonment of 8 days to 1 year, and to a fine of up to 5000 francs."

97. Michael Whine, "Expanding Holocaust Denial and Legislation Against it," *Jewish Political Studies Review* 20, no. 1 (Spring 2008): 62.

98. Section 26(1)a reads: "Anyone who publicly denies, disputes, approves or attempts to justify a Nazi, Communist or other genocide or Nazi, Communist or other crimes against humanity or war crimes or crimes against peace will be punished by imprisonment for six months to three years."

99. Talia Naamat, Nina Osin, and Dina Porat, eds., *Legislating for Equality: A Multinational Collection of Non-Discrimination Norms* (Leiden: Martinus Nijhoff, 2012), 117.

100. Clause 266(b) criminalizes: "publicly or with intent to disseminate to a wider circle, threaten, insult or degrade a group of persons on the basis of race, skin color, nationality, ethnicity, faith or sexual orientation."

101. Stavros Assimakopoulos, Fabienne H. Baider, and Sharon Millar, *Online Hate Speech in the European Union: A Discourse-Analytic Perspective* (Gewerbestrasse: Springer Open, 2017), 8.

102. Article 24(a) of the law of July 29, 1881, reads: "Anyone disputes the existence of one or more crimes against humanity such as they are defined by Article 6 of the statute of the international tribunal military annexed in the agreement of London of August 8, 1945 and which were carried out either by the members of an organization declared criminal pursuant to Article 9 of the aforementioned statute, or by a person found guilty such crimes by a French or international jurisdiction shall be punished by up to one year's imprisonment and a fine of 45000 Euros or one of those penalties only."

103. Ludovic Hennebel and Thomas Hochmann, eds., *Genocide Denials and the Law* (New York: Oxford University Press, 2011), 199.

104. Clause 130(1) reads: "Whosoever, in a manner capable of disturbing the public peace: 1. Incites hatred against segments of the population or calls for violent or arbitrary measures against them; or 2. Assaults the human dignity of others by insulting, maliciously maligning, or defaming segments of the population, shall be liable to imprisonment from three months to five years."

105. Clause 130(3) reads: "Whosoever publicly or in a meeting approves of, denies or downplays an act committed under the rule of National Socialism of the kind indicated in section 6 (1) of the Code of International Criminal Law, in a manner capable of disturbing the public peace shall be liable to imprisonment not exceeding five years or a fine." Clause 130(4) reads: "Whosoever publicly or in a meeting disturbs the public peace in a manner that violates the dignity of the victims by approving of, glorifying, or justifying National Socialist rule of arbitrary force shall be liable to imprisonment not exceeding three years or a fine."

106. Article 2 of the law 927/1979 reads: "Whoever intentionally, publicly, verbally or in print, over the internet or through any other medium or means, approves, ridicules or maliciously denies the existence or seriousness of crimes of genocide, war crimes, crimes against humanity, the Holocaust and other crimes of Nazism which have been recognised by decisions of international courts or the Hellenic Parliament and this behaviour is targeted against a group of people, or member thereof, which is identified on the basis of race, colour, religion, genealogical background, national or ethnic origins, sexual orientation, gender identity or disability, when this behaviour is expressed in a way that is capable of inciting violence or hatred or is of a threatening or insulting character against such a group or a member thereof, is subject to the penalties."

107. The law reads: "Those who publicly hurt the dignity of a victim of the Holocaust by denying or questioning the Holocaust itself, or claim it insignificant, infringe the law and can be punished by prison sentence of up to three years."

108. Benjamin Weinthal, "Hungary Passes Landmark Holocaust Denial Law," *Jerusalem Post*, March 19, 2010.

109. Article 3 talks about "the penalty of imprisonment from two to six years if the propaganda or the incitement committed so that there arises a real danger of diffusion, based in whole or in part on negating the Holocaust or genocide crimes, crimes against humanity and war crimes, as defined by articles 6, 7 and 8 of the statute of the International Criminal Court" (unofficial translation).

110. Piotr Bąkowski, *Holocaust Denial in Criminal Law: Legal Frameworks in Selected EU Member States* (Brussels: European Parliamentary Research Service, 2022), 7.

111. Article 405 reads: "Anyone who impedes or disturbs the exercise of functions, ceremonies or religious practices of the cult of a religious confession, which are carried out with the assistance of a minister of worship himself or in a place intended for worship, or in a place public or open to the public, he is punished with imprisonment of up to two years. If there are acts of violence against people or threats, imprisonment of one to three years applies."

112. Section 283 of criminal code reads: "Whoever publicly denies, coarsely trivializes, or tries to justify genocide or other crimes against humanity via word, writing,

pictures, electronically transmitted signs, gestures, violent acts or by other means shall be punished with imprisonment for up to two years."

113. Alessandro Perfetti, "Genocide Denial and Freedom of Expression" (master's thesis, LUISS Guido Carli, 2015/2016), 86.

114. Article 170(2) criminalizes "publicly condoning, denying or grossly trivializing (if done in a threatening, or insulting, or abusive manner or if it leads to a public order disturbance) of the USSR or Nazi Germany aggression against the Republic of Lithuania, the USSR or Nazi Germany genocide, crimes against humanity, or war crimes conducted against the citizens of the Republic of Lithuania or within its territory, or aggression against the Republic of Lithuania taking place in 1991-1992."

115. Elazar Barkan and Ariella Lang ed., *Memory Laws and Historical Justice: The Politics of Criminalizing the Past* (Cham: Palgrave Macmillan, 2022), 178.

116. Article 457(3) reads: "Anyone who has contested, minimized, justified or denied the existence of war crimes or crimes against humanity as defined in the statutes of the International Military Tribunal of 8 August 1945 or the existence of a genocide as defined by the Act of 8 August 1985 shall be punished with imprisonment of between 8 days and 6 months and/or a fine. A complaint must be lodged by the person against whom the offence was committed (victim or association) in order for proceedings to be brought."

117. Paola Gaeta, ed., *The UN Genocide Convention: A Commentary* (New York: Oxford University Press, 2009), 524.

118. Article 137(c) prohibits "deliberately giv[ing] public expression to views insulting to a group of persons on account of their race, religion, or conviction or sexual preference."

119. Ivan Hare and James Weinstein, eds., *Extreme Speech and Democracy* (New York: Oxford University Press, 2010), 58.

120. Article 55 reads: "He who publicly and contrary to facts contradicts the crimes mentioned in Article 1, clause 1 shall be subject to a fine or a penalty of deprivation of liberty of up to three years. The judgment shall be made publicly known." Article 1 reads: "This Act shall govern: 1. The registration, collection, access, management and use of the documents of the organs of state security created and collected between 22 July 1944 and 31 December 1989, and the documents of the organs of security of the Third Reich and the Union of Soviet Socialist Republics concerning: a) crimes perpetrated against persons of Polish nationality and Polish citizens of other ethnicity, nationalities in the period between 1 September 1939 and 31 December 1989: Nazi crimes, communist crimes, other crimes constituting crimes against peace, crimes against humanity or war crimes."

121. Uladzislau Belavusau, *Freedom of Speech: Importing European and US Constitutional Models in Transitional Democracies* (New York: Routledge, 2013), 192.

122. Article 257 reads: "Whoever publicly insults a group of people or individual person because of their national, ethnic, racial, religious, or because of its lack of religious beliefs or from such grounds violates the bodily integrity of another person, punishable by imprisonment of up to 3 years."

123. *ECRI Report on Portugal* (Strasbourg: Council of Europe, 2013), 10.

124. Article 5 reads: "Promoting the cult of persons guilty of committing a crime against peace and humanity or promoting fascist, racist or xenophobic ideology, through propaganda, committed by any means, in public, is punishable with imprisonment from 3 months to 3 years and the loss of some rights." Article 6 reads: "The public denial of the holocaust or its effects constitutes offense and punishable by imprisonment from 6 months to 5 years and the loss of rights" (unofficial translation).

125. Section 422d reads: "Who(ever) publicly denies, denies, approves or tries to justify the Holocaust, crimes of regimes based on fascist ideology, crimes of regimes based on communist ideology or crimes of other similar movements that use violence, the threat of violence or the threat of other serious harm with the aim of suppressing the fundamental rights and freedoms of persons shall be punished by imprisonment of six months to three years."

126. Assaf Uni, "Spanish Court Rules Out Jail Sentences for Holocaust Denial," *Haaretz*, November 9, 2007.

127. Article 261 reads: "Anyone who publicly degrades or discriminates, verbally, in writing, in images, in gestures, acts or in any other way, against a person or a group of people because of their race, ethnicity or religion in a manner contrary to human dignity or for any reason against genocide or other crimes against humanity denies, grossly trivializes or tries to justify, [...] is punished with imprisonment up to three years or a fine."

128. Richard Seymour, "Azhar Ahmed – Charged with Treason Over Facebook Comments?" *Guardian*, March 15, 2012.

129. Jerome Taylor, "Azhar Ahmed, A Tasteless Facebook Update, and More Evidence of Britain's Terrifying New Censorship," *Independent*, October 9, 2012.

Chapter Three

Muslims and the Freedom of Religion in Europe

A BRIEF HISTORY OF MUSLIMS IN EUROPE

By middle of the seventh century Islam had reached a region of Caucasian populations that would later become part of Russia, but the first genuine foothold of Muslims in Europe was the Umayyad conquest of the Iberian Peninsula in 711. Muslims renamed this land as Al-Andalusia. By the tenth century, most of the population of present-day Portugal and Spain had willingly converted to Islam.[1] Muslims then raided Rome in 846 and the Emirate of Sicily was established in 965. Subsequently, they also kept losing control and were confined to establish Emirate of Granada in 1230 that lasted until 1492. But by 1480, there were several Muslim majority territories present in Europe (see figure 3.1).

The Ottomans conquered the Balkans and crossed into Europe after 1354. Constantinople fell into their hands in 1453. The Ottomans stretched northward and reached Hungary in the sixteenth century and Podolia (or Podilia) in the mid-seventeenth century. The empire conquered present-day Greece, Bulgaria, Romania, Albania, Serbia, Macedonia, Montenegro, Bosnia, and Hungary and parts of present-day Croatia, Slovenia, and Serbia.[2]

With the defeat in the Great Turkish War in 1699, Ottoman expansion in Europe ended resulting in the gradual loss of control over almost all of its European territories leaving a considerable number of Muslims in various parts under its rule.[3] The Ottoman Empire collapsed in 1923. In the latter part of the twentieth century large numbers of Muslims from different parts of the world began immigrating to Europe. Most Muslims came from the former colonies of European states as laborers and to find other jobs for better living.

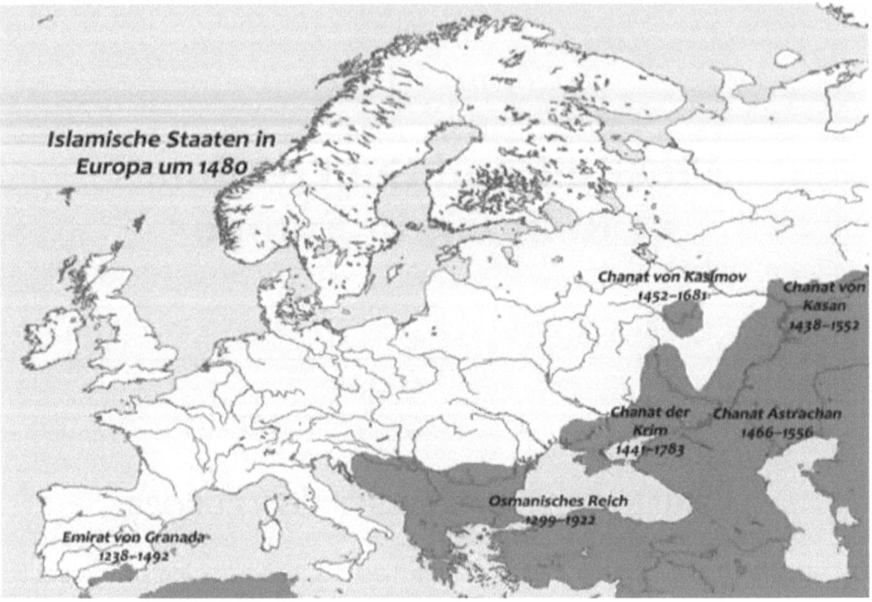

Figure 3.1. Islamic states in Europe around 1480.
Source: Leibniz Institute of European History (2012).

CURRENT MUSLIM DEMOGRAPHY AND FUTURE PROJECTIONS

Although there are no authentic numbers available to determine the size of the Muslim community in Europe as a whole, data of the Muslim population in different European countries shows that adherents of Islam constitute the second largest religious group in the continent after Christianity. Russia was estimated to have twenty-three million Muslims in 2005 with rapid growth[4] constituting the largest Muslim group in Europe with 11.7 percent population. Muslims comprised 6 percent of the total population of Europe in 2010. Out of this, nineteen million (i.e., 3.8 million of population) were living in the European Union. By 2030, it is predicted that Muslims will make up 8 percent of the total European population , that is, from 44.1 million to 58.2 million[5] and 10.2 percent by 2050 making Islam the fastest growing religion on the continent with a 63 percent increase in the number of adherents.[6] Turks living outside Turkey but in Europe constitute the biggest immigrant Muslim group on the continent as a whole.[7] However, in transcontinental countries, Turkey and Azerbaijan have the biggest Muslim population with 98 percent and 96.9 percent, respectively. These figures show that almost all major western European and Nordic countries have a Muslim population size of 5–10 percent, which is growing rapidly. Studies have

Table 3.1. Muslim Population in European Countries

Country	*Percentage*	*Country*	*Percentage*
Bulgaria	11.1%	Germany	6.1%
France	8.8%	Switzerland	6.1%
Sweden	8.1%	Norway	5.7%
Belgium	7.6%	Greece	5.7%
Netherlands	7.1%	Denmark	5.4%
Austria	6.9%	Italy	4.8%
UK	6.3%		

Source: "Europe's Growing Muslim Population." Pew Research Center, Washington, D.C. (November 29, 2017)

also estimated that Muslims can become 14 percent of the European population by 2050 in a case of a high migration scenario.[8] Recently, major controversies relating to Islam and Muslims also emerged in some of these countries. Muslims are a subject of debate in almost every country.

Among these countries, Germany is the most populous on the continent after Russia with almost 10 percent of Europe's whole population.[9] It is followed by France with 7.88 percent[10] and the United Kingdom with 7.88 percent,[11] while Denmark has 6.68 percent of the total European population.[12] Table 3.2 shows the estimated growth of Muslims in Europe by 2050 under a "zero migration scenario."

Table 3.2. Estimated Growth of Muslims in Europe

Country	*Percentage*	*Country*	*Percentage*
France	12.7%	Netherlands	9.1%
Bulgaria	12.5%	Germany	8.7%
Sweden	11.1%	Italy	8.3%
Belgium	11.1%	Switzerland	8.2%
UK	9.7%	Denmark	7.6%
Austria	9.3%	Norway	7.2%

Source: "Europe's Growing Muslim Population." Pew Research Center, Washington, D.C. (November 29, 2017)

FREEDOM OF RELIGION AND MUSLIMS

Freedom of religion has remained a complex matter throughout human history. Until modern times, *cuius regio eius religio*, a Latin phrase meaning one who rules the region decides the religion, was practiced throughout Europe. It was practiced as a general rule established by the Peace of Augsburg in 1555.[13]

In modern times, the Universal Declaration of Human Rights 1948, the Arcot Krishnaswami Study 1959, the International Covenants on Human Rights 1966 (in particular the International Covenant on Civil and Political Rights), and the Declaration on the Elimination of All Forms of Intolerance and Discrimination Based on Religion or Belief 1981 gradually developed the concept of freedom of religion on a global level. The European Convention on Human Rights 1950 laid foundations of such legislation on the continent with its Article 9 guaranteeing freedom of thought, conscience, and religion.[14]

The same article[15] provides limitations to this freedom as well. The OSCE Joint Declaration on Defamation of Religions and the Anti-Terrorism and Anti-Extremism Legislation 2008[16] sheds light on the complicated relationship of the freedom of expression with freedom of religion. It states that limitations to freedom of expressions should be capped when talking about specific institutions, notions, and beliefs. The Charter of Fundamental Rights of the European Union 2012[17] also secures freedom of religion. The Council of the European Union Directive on equal opportunities of employment also forbids discrimination on the basis of religion.

Despite effective legal instruments and productive policies to integrate Muslims, Europe has not been successful in doing so especially after 9/11. While

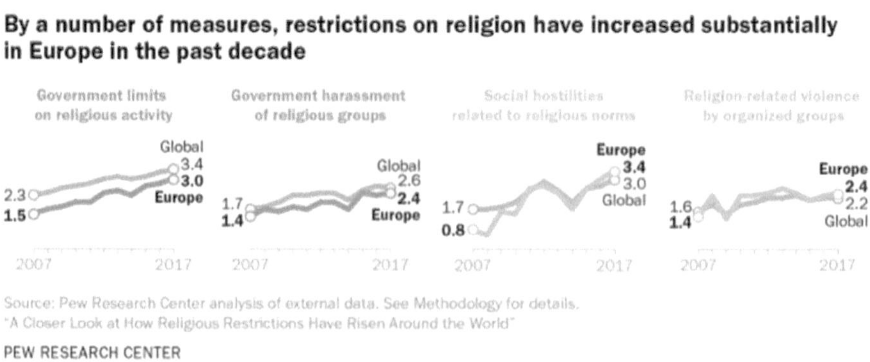

Figure 3.2. Restrictions on religion in Europe.

Source: "Europe experienced a surge in government restrictions on religious activity over the last decade" Pew Research Center, Washington, D.C. (July 29, 2019). https://www.pewresearch.org/fact-tank/2019/07/29/europe-experienced-a-surge-in-government-restrictions-on-religious-activity-over-the-last-decade/

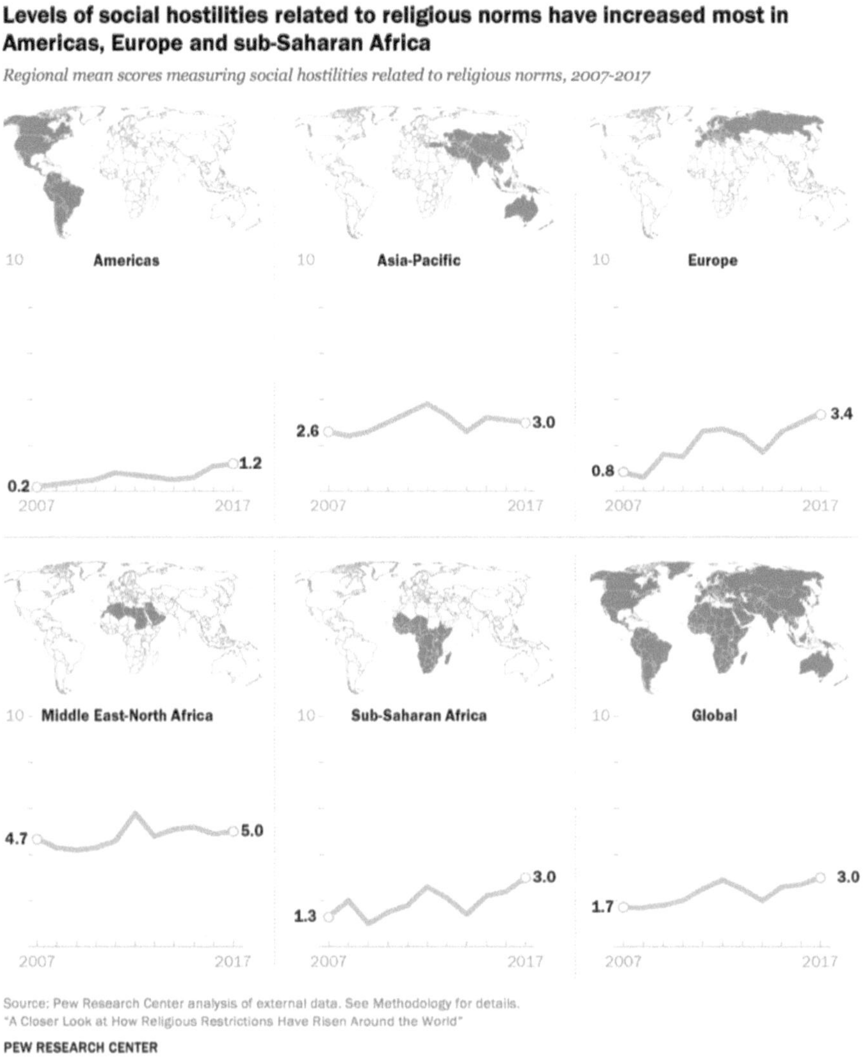

Figure 3.3. Religious restrictions around the world.

Source: "A Closer Look at How Religious Restrictions Have Risen Around the World" Pew Research Center, Washington, D.C. (July 15, 2019). https://www.pewresearch.org religion/2019/07/15/a-closer-look-at-how-religious-restrictions-have-risen-around-the-world/

the European media is vigilant to report discrimination against Muslims too, a 2012 study revealed that Muslims faced the highest degree of discrimination in the media in countries like France, Germany, and the United Kingdom.[18] The British media has long been accused of spreading hate speech against

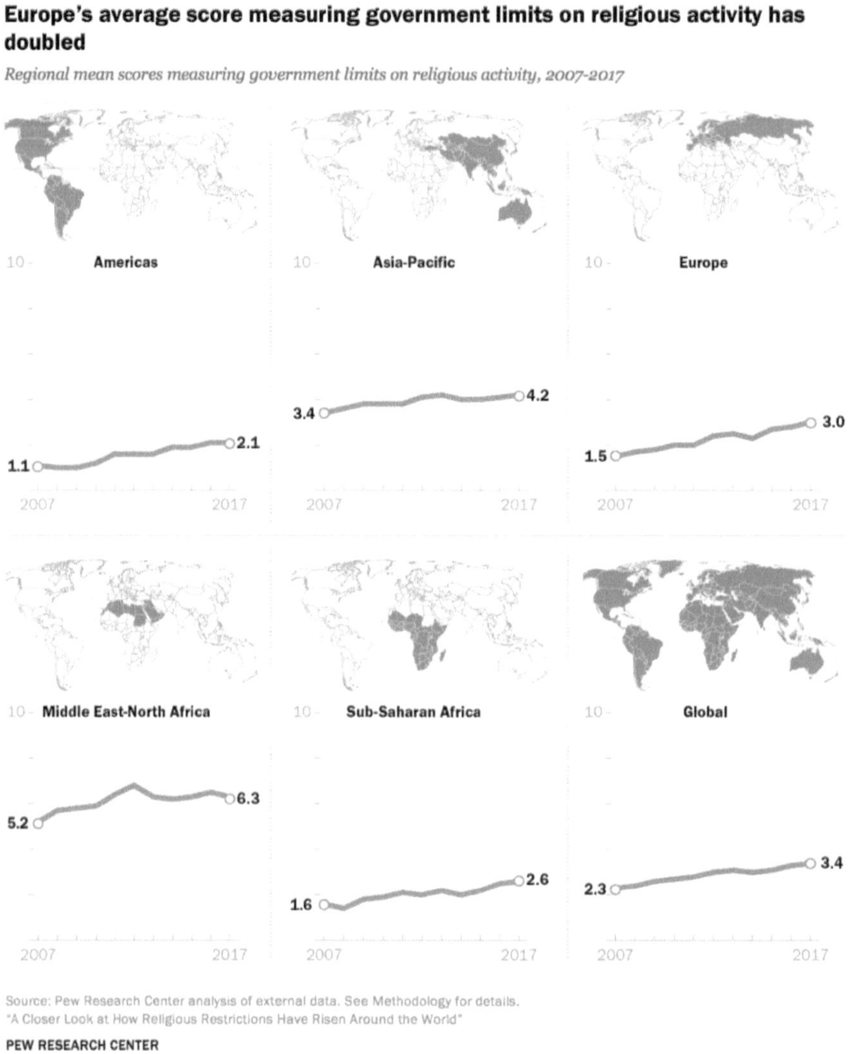

Figure 3.4. Government limits on religious activity in Europe.

Source: "A Closer Look at How Religious Restrictions Have Risen Around the World" Pew Research Center, Washington, D.C. (July 15, 2019). https://www.pewresearch.org/religion/2019/07/15/a-closer-look-at-how-religious-restrictions-have-risen-around-the-world/

Muslims.[19] Scholars also note that what the Muslims face in some European societies is a result of their media portrayal as being "barbaric, irrational, primitive and sexist."[20]

It was observed in 2012 that there were about 190 anti-Muslim outfits in Europe and North America. The same ideology "inspired" extremists like

Anders Behring Breivik who confessed to the July 2011 mass shooting in Norway. Those killings were justified by the murderer "as part of a 'war' between the West and Islamists."[21] In 2016, the harassment of religious minorities by nationalist groups and politicians saw a sharp increase in Europe having Muslims being the primary target. Nationalist parties in 33 percent of European countries gave statements against religious minorities targeting Muslims in most cases with derogatory remarks or policies.[22]

Among the European states individually, Austria does not have any state religion, but it recognizes sixteen religious societies. According to the Basic Law on the General Rights of Citizens, everyone is free to practice any religion[23] but unrecognized groups cannot worship[24] in public. Islam was recognized in 1912 and Muslims constitute the second largest group after Christianity. The state introduced new Islam Law in 2015 to promote better cohabitation but sentiments against Islam are on the rise and 2018 saw a 75 percent increase in anti-Muslim incidents. The government-partner Freedom Party of Austria (Freiheitliche Partei Österreichs; FPÖ) is specifically accused of having an anti-Islamic agenda.[25]

The Belgian constitution *Grondwet* guarantees freedom of worship through Article 19[26] under the ambit of state law and bars the state from intervening in religious matters under Article 21[27] of the constitution. However, the government continues its policy of curbing "radical Islam" and controversies keep generating on Muslim headscarf bans and prohibition of animal slaughtering. Anti-Muslim incidents have also increased during recent years.[28]

Denmark, through its constitution, recognizes the Evangelical Lutheran Church as the state church[29] that receives subsidies from the government and the monarch has to be a member of the state church.[30] The constitution guarantees freedom of worship[31] but the country is often criticized for being intolerant toward Muslims. Nye Borgerlige, or "The New Right" Party is openly critical of Islam and hate crimes against Muslims have seen an increase. Anti-Muslim statements were also made by the immigration and integration minster.[32] On January 20, 2016, the city council in Randers passed a bill to make pork mandatory in public institutions including schools.[33] In July 2018, the British newspaper *The Guardian* wrote an editorial after Denmark passed a "ghetto law" and called Danish policies "xenophobic," "racist," and "discriminating" against Muslims.[34] Rights activists in Denmark termed this law "explicitly Islamophobic" and a "betrayal of Danish tolerant values."[35] Parliament considered banning circumcision in September 2018, which was criticized by Jews and Muslims alike.[36] The custom of shaking hands to get citizenship was also criticized as Muslim-specific and there are few instances when Muslims were denied citizenship when they refused to shake hands. Even several Danish mayors demanded an end to this law.[37]

The Evangelical Lutheran Church of Finland and the Finnish Orthodox Church receive state funding and can also levy taxes. By law, it is the responsibility of the state to provide "comprehensive religious education." The

Evangelical Church enjoyed the status of state church until 1870, but it is now considered a "folk church" since after the first freedom of religion law was passed in 1922. Article 6[38] of the constitution of Finland guarantees equal opportunities for every citizen irrespective of religion while Article 11[39] gives the right to freedom of religion. However, some politicians openly make critical remarks against Muslims and the Ministry of Justice advised the government to ban circumcision, which has been debated by parliament as well.[40]

France officially separated church and state on January 1, 1906, and Articles 1 and 2 of the law passed on December 9, 1905, clearly state this. But at the same time, Article 12 of the same law says that religious buildings shall be state property and Article 13[41] renders those establishments to "exercise of worship" free of charge. This means that the religious buildings existing in 1905 are still being run by taxpayers' funds. Since there was no religious building present at that time other than of Christianity, so the said law is blamed to be discriminatory and the French government assured in 2018 that it is trying to end this discrimination especially in the Muslim context.[42] However, constitutionally, France is a secular state[43] with no distinction on the basis of religion. While French government tries to protect Muslims and condemns anti-Islamic sentiments, hatred against Muslims remains a problem. President Emmanuel Macron termed *Salafism* and extremism "a problem" and a UN rapporteur said in 2018 that the government was treating Muslims as "suspect community" and curbing their religious freedom by shutting down mosques.[44]

Article 137 of the German constitution clearly states that there will be no state church and Article 4 guarantees[45] freedom of faith and conscience. However, the federal interior minister in March of 2018 said that Germany is "characterized by Christianity" and Islam is not part of national culture. In May of the same year, the Bavarian government ordered crosses to be placed at all public buildings in a "clearly visible" manner. Patriotic Europeans against the Islamization of the Occident (Patriotische Europäer gegen die Islamisierung des Abendlandes PEGIDA) also stages anti-Islamic protests while the Alternative for Germany Party (Alternative für Deutschland, AfD) continues to make anti-Islamic statements and hate crimes and far-right demonstrations against Muslims are also continued.[46]

In Italy, too, there is no state religion, the Catholic Church is sovereign but separate from the state[47] and all religions are equal[48] before the law. However, the specific mentioning in the constitution gives special status to the Catholic Church that other religious denominations do not enjoy. Twelve other religious denominations enjoy benefits under an agreement with the state, but Muslims being deprived of this face difficulties including being unable to build mosques. Hate crimes against Muslims are on the rise especially against children in schools. In April 2018, a pig's head was thrown into a building designated by Muslims to be a worship place. Deputy prime minister and League (Lega) Party leader made anti-Islamic statements along with several other political leaders.[49]

The constitution of the Netherlands in its Article 6[50] gives every citizen the right to freely profess any religion, but the country has seen substantial anti-Islamic sentiments after 9/11. Violence and hatred against Muslims continue and several politicians make statements critical of Islam,[51] most prominent being Geert Wilders who is the leader of the Party for Freedom (Partij voor de Vrijheid, PVV). There have been attacks on mosques, and by 2015 40 percent of the mosques were attacked or vandalized. Dutch courts convicted several persons and declared the attacks as terrorism.[52]

Same as Denmark, the Norwegian monarch has to be Evangelical-Lutheran[53] and the state gives priority and benefits to the Evangelical-Lutheran Church as the Established Church of Norway.[54] Despite this, the constitution talks of equality of all religions.[55] There have been hate crimes against Muslims and some anti-Islamic organizations are also active. Far-right NDL (Norwegian Defense League) works closely with EDL (English Defense League) and 2011 shooting convict Anders Behring Breivik was having close links with the same.[56] In 2016, a hairdresser who happened to be member of the anti-Islamic organization PEGIDA refused a hijab-wearing client and was fined by the court.[57, 58] An anti-immigrant group was criticized in 2017 for a Facebook post mistaking empty bus seats as burqa-clad Muslim women.[59] A right-wing sympathizer stormed an Oslo mosque with arms in August 2019[60] and in November of the same year the leader of Stop Islamization of Norway (SIAN) Lars Thorson tried to burn the Qur'an during an anti-Islam rally in Kristiansand city.[61] Political rhetoric against Muslims is also present among several parties and even the prime minister is blamed of maintaining a "calculated ambiguity" on the issue.[62]

The Swedish constitution safeguards freedom to practice religion.[63] It mentions the Church of Sweden more than once, but separation of the church and state took place in 2000. However, the SAP (Social Democratic Party), SD (Sweden Democrats), and V (Left Party) are prominent in making anti-immigrant moves and statements. There have been calls by politicians to stop Muslim call to prayer, circumcision of boys, wearing the hijab in schools, and independent religious schools, etc. Threats to Muslims were also increasing according to a 2017 survey.[64]

The Federal Constitution of the Swiss Confederation guarantees freedom of religion and conscience[65] but still Muslims face religious discrimination. Rows over Muslim slaughtering of animals continues, and the "Swiss Stop Islam Award" was announced by an activist in Ticino Canton in 2018.[66] In Lausanne, a Muslim couple was denied Swiss citizenship in 2018 after they refused to shake hands with members of the opposite sex.[67]

In United Kingdom, Article 13[68] of the Human Rights Act 1998 guarantees freedom of religion in line with the European Convention on Human Rights. However, the Church of England is the established church in England and the supreme governor of which is the reigning monarch with authority to make important appointments. Two archbishops and twenty-four bishops sit in the House of Lords and are called Lords Spiritual.[69] The Church of Scotland (Kirk) is the national Church of Scotland since 1690.[70] Discrimination and hatred against Islam is now a longstanding problem in the United Kingdom and violence, threats, and vandalism, etc. continue.[71, 72] In 2019, a white supremacist was jailed for running "Punish a Muslim Day" campaign.[73] Islamophobia is said to have become "part and parcel" of politics and the Conservative Party, especially its ex-leader and former prime minister Boris Johnson is accused of spreading anti-Muslim sentiments. He compared burqa-wearing Muslim women with "letterboxes," "bank robbers," said "Islam is the problem,"[74] but refused to apologize despite several demands.[75]

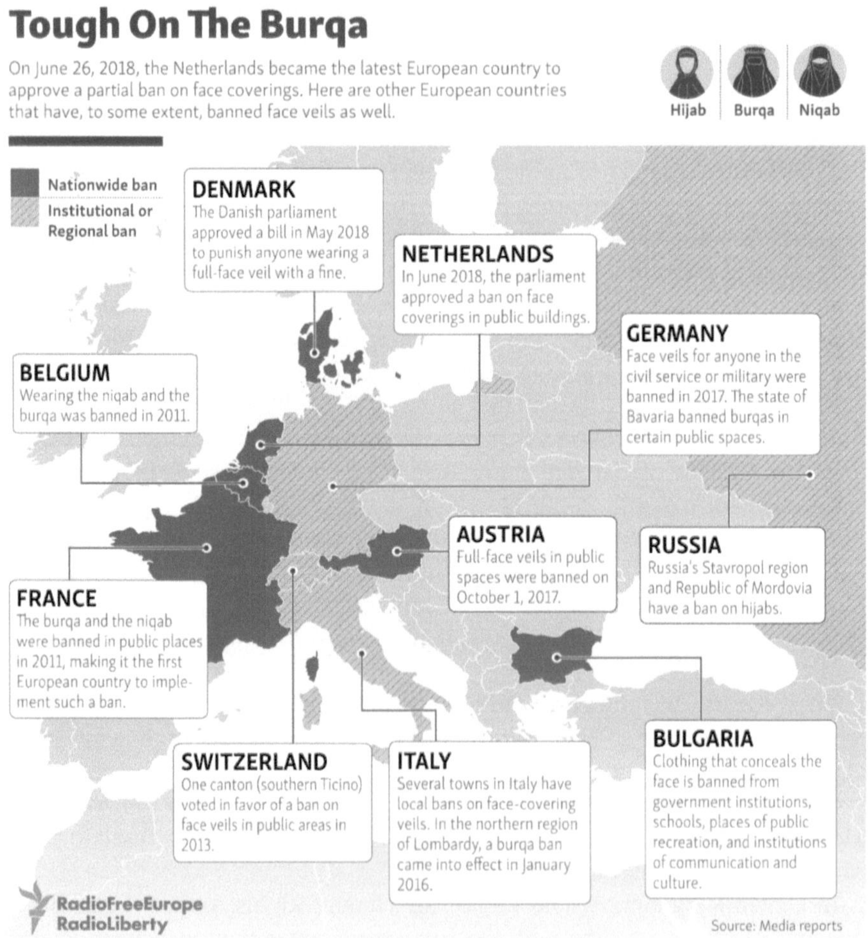

Figure 3.5. European countries with burqa ban (June 2018).

Source: https://www.rferl.org/a/tough-on-the-burqa/28274539.html

LIMITATIONS TO MUSLIM EXPRESSIONS

According to a survey, 50 percent of the citizens of fifteen mostly western European countries were of the view that Muslim women should not be allowed to wear a veil that covers their face. On the other hand, 23 percent of those are completely against any religious clothing for Muslim women.[76]

On October 1, 2017, Austria placed a ban on the hiding of faces at public places and buildings[77] with a fine of up to 150 euros. The ban was informally called the "burqa ban" throughout and perceived to be particularly against Muslim women. The interior ministry leaflet also had a sketch of a Muslim woman and writings in Arabic that showed whom it was directed to.[78]

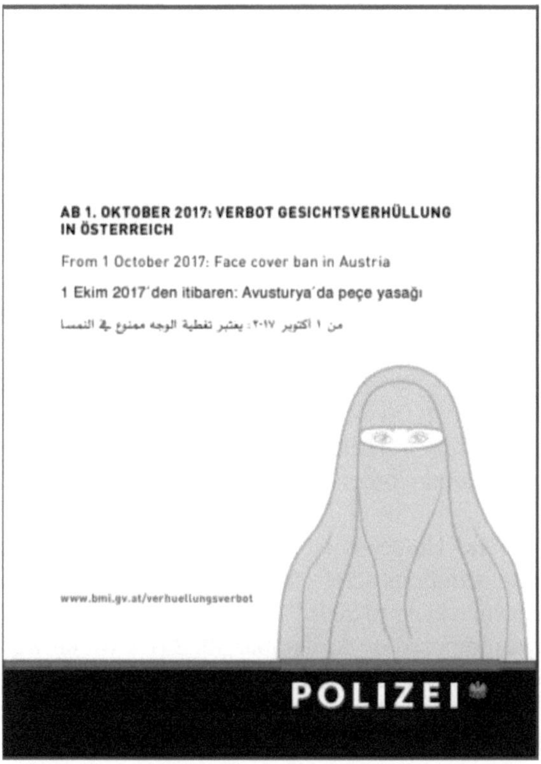

Figure 3.6. Face cover ban in Austria from October 1, 2017.

Source: https://www.bmi.gv.at/verhuellungsverbot

Austrian Muslim groups protested against the Muslim-specific ban as the government had warned the Muslim women prior to banning that they should adhere to it.[79] On the very first day of the ban, a Muslim woman was forced by the police to remove her veil in public.[80] According to an estimate, only 100 to 150 women used to cover their face in entire Austria when the prohibition came into force. Local police said that full face coverings were causing no problems and research showed that only four charges were found accurate during six months and all were against a single woman.[81] The president of the Austrian Bar Association termed this approach "bad and wrong"[82] and most interestingly, the federal president himself termed it "not a good law"[83] and called all women to wear headscarves to fight "rampant Islamophobia."[84] Incidents of harassment, quarrel, and attempted assaults also took place when individuals wanted to enforce this so called burqa ban.[85]

On May 15, 2019, wearing headscarves in primary schools was banned and governing center-right People's Party (ÖVP) and the far-right Freedom Party (FPÖ) explicitly said that it was against Muslims. The Austrian Muslim community called it "shameless" and a "direct assault" on Muslims. The media also called it Muslim-specific as Sikh *patka* and Jewish *kippa* were exempted from a ban on headscarves in Austrian primary schools.[86]

In Belgium, the municipality of Maaseik banned the burqa in 2004 while Antwerp did the same in 2005.[87] A bill was tabled in the Belgian lower house of parliament and was passed on April 29, 2010, prohibiting anything that hides the identity of the wearer at public places with a penalty of fifteen to twenty-five euros or seven days in jail. Strongly condemned by Amnesty International, the bill could not come into force due to the subsequent dissolution of parliament.[88] At that time, around only thirty women used to wear that sort of veil in a Muslim population of almost half a million.[89] By 2011, the ban on face coverings was in place in several Belgian municipalities and a local court declared such ban illegal on January 26, 2011.[90] On July 23, 2011, the burqa was banned with punishment of 137.50 euros fine and seven days sentence. The European Court of Human Rights upheld the ban on July 11, 2017, but when the ban took effect in 2011, it was criticized by a parliamentarian citing that only an estimated two hundred to three hundred women were wearing that sort of veil in the whole country.[91]

On February 7, 2016, Bosnia and Herzegovina banned religious symbols, including headscarves in judicial institutions across the country.[92]

A Bulgarian town banned face veils in April 2016[93] and a countrywide ban on wearing veils in public places was imposed on September 30, 2016, which was condemned by Amnesty International as a violation of the "freedom of expression and religion."[94]

In Denmark, a ban on burqas and niqabs came into force on August 1, 2018, which was passed by the parliament on May 31 if the same year. Violators would pay 1,000 kroner for the first time and up to 10,000 kroner for repeated attempts with a sentence up to six months. According to research, only two hundred Muslim women used to wear such a veil in Denmark at that time.[95] Debate on Muslim veils in Denmark started in April 2006 when twenty-four-year-old Asmaa Abdol-Hamid appeared on TV in a hijab.[96]

France placed a ban on wearing any religious symbols in state schools on September 2, 2004, but it was thought and reported as Muslim-specific.[97] French lower house legislators voted for this ban in February and President Jacques Chirac had to issue a statement on Islam and Secularism in these words: "Today, all the great religions in the history of France have adapted themselves to that principle [of secularism]. For the most recently arrived, I'm speaking here of Islam, secularism is a chance, the chance to be a religion of France."[98] Human Rights Watch termed this ban discriminatory and a violation of religious freedom[99] while the United States Commission on International Religious Freedom also expressed concerns on this legislation.[100] On October 9, 2008, Muslim women wearing a burqa were barred from taking state language classes.[101]

Veils that cover the face, including burqas, got banned across the country on September 15, 2010, with a fine of 150 euros and/or a citizenship course. Forcing to wear a niqab or burqa would result in a year of imprisonment or a fine of 15,000 euros. With this, France became the first state in Europe to ban face coverings on a countrywide level. The French Council of State, however, warned this could be repugnant to the national constitution and international human rights laws.[102] But on July 1, 2014, the European Court of Human Rights upheld the decision.[103] The UN Human Rights Committee said that the rights of Muslim women were violated by a national ban on face coverings in France and the said law "disproportionately harmed" the women practicing Islam in that country.[104] The so called burkini was banned on nearly thirty French coastal sites and respective mayors refused to lift the same despite a court ruling against it.[105]

In Germany, the federal constitutional court allowed Afghan-born teacher on September 24, 2003, to wear an Islamic scarf in school when half of the regions in the country banned teachers from wearing headscarves.[106] Even German churches did not agree with the ban.[107] On January 15, 2004, then president Johannes Rau expressed his deep concern over discrimination against Muslims and not treating them equally as other religious groups in the country. He said, "Banning headscarves from schools for being a mark of religious identification makes it very difficult to defend the wearing of monk's habits."[108] On March 13, 2015, the country's highest constitutional court ruled against an absolute headscarf ban on women teachers,[109] but by the end of 2016 German chancellor Angela Merkel was determined to ban face veils "wherever legally possible."[110]

In 2017, the German parliament favored a ban on face coverings in the judiciary, civil service, and military,[111] but on September 22, 2017, the upper house approved the ban on face coverings while driving.[112] In the same year, the state of Bavaria banned face veils in educational institutions and other civil services.[113] Full face covering was banned in classrooms by Kiel University on February 13, 2019, while nothing was said about other religious symbols, which attracted criticism from different circles terming this "untenable" and "nothing to do with education."[114] On February 3, 2020, a local court in Hamburg permitted a sixteen-year-old girl to wear a niqab in class, again generating debate on the issue in the country.[115]

In the Lombardy region of Italy, on January 1, 2016, a ban on wearing the burqa and Islamic veils at government buildings and hospitals was put into place.[116]

In Kosovo, headscarves in public schools were banned nationwide from April 14, 2010.[117] In Latvia, a national ban was put in place on April 21, 2016, prohibiting face veils despite the fact that only three women used to wear that across the country, according to an estimate.[118] Luxembourg's parliament passed a law on April 27, 2018, that criminalized face coverings at certain public places.[119] In Moldova, Muslims were barred from offering prayer publicly in March 2013, a move called "discriminatory" by Amnesty International.[120]

The Netherlands declared face coverings illegal in public places and transport on August 1, 2019, and punishable with a fine of 150 to 415 euros. The mayor of Amsterdam expressed her disagreement as only one hundred Muslim women were regularly wearing such veils at that time.[121] Far-right anti-Islamic politician Geert Wilders introduced this ban in 2005.[122] Apart from Dutch Muslims and rights activists, a UN rapporteur on racism also criticized the ban while Human Rights Watch termed it controversial.[123]

On June 6, 2018, the Norwegian national parliament voted for a countrywide ban on full or partial face coverings in all schools and universities. Educational institutions and national student unions criticized the ban.[124]

On June 15, 2010, the Spanish city of Barcelona banned full face veils at some public places while many other parts of the country were subsequently slapping burqa bans at a pace that has been described by the then immigration minister as "more bans than burqas." Spain's senate demanded the government to ban burqas and niqabs in a manner that does not affect Christian *nazarenos.*[125]

The Swedish municipality of Staffanstorp placed a ban on head coverings on May 29, 2019,[126] followed by the municipality of Skurup against which non-Muslim teachers protested by wearing headscarves.[127] The Swedish court later declared this ban illegal.[128]

The constitution in Switzerland was amended on November 29, 2009, after a popular vote to ban the construction of minarets. Article 72 reads that "the construction of minarets is prohibited" without giving any elaboration. Fifty-seven percent of the voters in a national referendum nodded to ban construction of minarets. It was a move termed as "defamation of religions" by the Human Rights Council of UN General Assembly in a resolution.[129] On September 23, 2018, citizens in the Swiss canton of St. Gallen voted for a ban on face coverings becoming the second canton after Ticino to implement similar restriction in 2013.[130]

In the United Kingdom, schools were given the right to decide on face veils of students considering several conditions. This happened on March 20, 2007, after a female student lost her case in court against a niqab ban at her school.[131]

NOTES

1. Albert Hourani, *A History of the Arab Peoples* (London: Faber & Faber, 2002), 42.

2. Virginia Aksan, *Ottoman Wars, 1700–1860: An Empire Besieged* (London: Pearson Education Ltd., 2007), 133–35.

3. Thomas Walker Arnold, *The Preaching of Islam: History of the Propagation of the Muslim Faith* (Westminster: Archibald Constable & Co., 1896), 135–44.

4. "The Rise of Russian Muslims Worries Orthodox Church," *Times*, August 5, 2005.

5. "The Future of the Global Muslim Population Projections for 2010-2030," Pew Forum, January 27, 2011.

6. "Religious Composition by Country, 2010–2050," Pew Forum, April 2, 2015.

7. Jeffrey E. Cole, ed., *Ethnic Groups of Europe: An Encyclopedia* (Santa Barbara, CA: ABC-CLIO, 2011), 367.

8. "Europe's Growing Muslim Population," Pew Forum, November 29, 2017.

9. "Population by Sex and Citizenship," Statistisches Bundesamt, accessed April 1, 2020, https://www.destatis.de/EN/FactsFigures/SocietyState/Population/CurrentPopulation/Tables/Census_SexAndCitizenship.html.

10. "2016 Demographic Review," Institut National De La Statistique et Des Études Économiques, January 17, 2017, accessed April 1, 2020, https://www.insee.fr/fr/statistiques/2554860.

11. "Population Estimates," Office for National Statistics, accessed April 1, 2020, https://www.ons.gov.uk/peoplepopulationandcommunity/populationandmigration/populationestimates.

12. "Denmark in Figures 2018," Statistics Denmark, accessed April 1, 2020, https://www.dst.dk/en/Statistik/Publikationer/VisPub?cid=28923.

13. Stephen D. Krasner, *Sovereignty Organized Hypocrisy* (Princeton, NJ: Princeton University Press. 1999), 79.

14. Article 9 reads: "Everyone has the right to freedom of thought, conscience and religion; this right includes freedom to change his religion or belief and freedom, either alone or in community with others and in public or private, to manifest his religion or belief, in worship, teaching, practice and observance."

15. "Freedom to manifest one's religion or beliefs shall be subject only to such limitations as are prescribed by law and are necessary in a democratic society in the interests of public safety, for the protection of public order, health or morals, or for the protection of the rights and freedoms of others."

16. The Defamation of Religions part reads: "The concept of 'defamation of religions' does not accord with international standards regarding defamation, which refer

to the protection of reputation of individuals, while religions, like all beliefs, cannot be said to have a reputation of their own. Restrictions on freedom of expression should be limited in scope to the protection of overriding individual rights and social interests, and should never be used to protect particular institutions, or abstract notions, concepts or beliefs, including religious ones. Restrictions on freedom of expression to prevent intolerance should be limited in scope to advocacy of national, racial or religious hatred that constitutes incitement to discrimination, hostility or violence."

17. Article 10 reads: "1. Everyone has the right to freedom of thought, conscience and religion. This right includes freedom to change religion or belief and freedom, either alone or in community with others and in public or in private, to manifest religion or belief, in worship, teaching, practice and observance. 2. The right to conscientious objection is recognised, in accordance with the national laws governing the exercise of this right."

18. J. R. Kunst, D. L. Sam, and P. Ulleberg, "Perceived Islamophobia: Scale Development and Validation," *International Journal of Intercultural Relations* 37, no. 2 (March 2013): 225–37.

19. John E. Richardson, *(Mis)representing Islam: The Racism and Rhetoric of British Broadsheet Newspapers* (Amsterdam: John Benjamins Publishing Company, 2004), 15.

20. H. A. Jawad and Tansin Benn, eds., *Women and Gender, the Middle East and the Islamic World*, vol. 2 of *Muslim Women in the United Kingdom and Beyond: Experiences and Images* (Leiden, Netherlands: Brill Academic Publishers, 2003), 165.

21. Mark Townsend, "Far-Right Anti-Muslim Network on Rise Globally as Breivik Trial Opens," *Guardian*, April 14, 2012.

22. "Global Uptick in Government Restrictions on Religion in 2016," Pew Forum, June 21, 2018.

23. Article 14 reads: "Everyone is guaranteed complete freedom of belief and conscience. The enjoyment of civil and political rights is independent of religious beliefs; however, the civic duties must not be interrupted by the religion. No one can be compelled to perform an ecclesiastical act or to take part in an ecclesiastical ceremony, unless he is subject to the force of another person authorized by law." Article 15 reads: "Every legally recognized church and religious society has the right of common public religious practice, organizes and administers its internal affairs independently, remains in the possession and enjoyment of its institutions, foundations and funds intended for cultural, educational and charitable purposes, but is, like every society, subject to general state laws."

24. Article 16 reads: "The followers of a religion not legally recognized are allowed to practice the religion at home, provided that it is neither illegal nor morality-violating."

25. *Austria 2018 International Religious Freedom Report* (Washington, DC: US Department of State, 2018), 1.

26. It reads: "Freedom of worship, its public practice and freedom to demonstrate one's opinions on all matters are guaranteed, but offences committed when this freedom is used may be punished."

27. It reads: "The State does not have the right to intervene either in the appointment or in the installation of ministers of any religion whatsoever or to forbid these

ministers from corresponding with their superiors, from publishing the acts of these superiors, but, in this latter case, normal responsibilities as regards the press and publishing apply."

28. *Belgium 2018 International Religious Freedom Report* (Washington, DC: US Department of State, 2018), 1.

29. Section 4 reads: "The Evangelical Lutheran Church shall be the Established Church of Denmark, and as such shall be supported by the State."

30. Section 6 reads: "The King shall be a member of the Evangelical Lutheran Church."

31. Section 67 reads: "Citizens shall be at liberty to form congregations for the worship of God in a manner which is in accordance with their convictions, provided that nothing contrary to good morals or public order shall be taught or done." Section 68 reads: "No one shall be liable to make personal contributions to any denomination other than the one to which he adheres." Section 70 reads: "No person shall by reason of his creed or descent be deprived of access to the full enjoyment of civic and political rights, nor shall he escape compliance with any common civic duty for such reasons."

32. *Denmark 2018 International Religious Freedom Report* (Washington, DC: US Department of State, 2018), 1.

33. Alexandra Sims, "Danish Town Says Public Institutions Must Serve Pork as Country's 'Meatball War' Continues," *Independent*, January 20, 2016.

34. Editorial, "The Guardian View on Forcible Integration in Denmark: This Cannot End Well," *Guardian*, July 8, 2018.

35. Michala Bendixen, "Denmark's 'anti-Ghetto' Laws Are a Betrayal of Our Tolerant Values," *Guardian*, July 10, 2018.

36. "Danish Parliament Committee Approves Draft Resolution to Ban Circumcision," *Haaretz*, September 30, 2018.

37. "Danish Mayors Call for Scrapping of Citizenship Handshake Law," *The Local* (Denmark), September 12, 2019.

38. It reads: "People are equal before the law. No one shall be placed in a different position on the basis of sex, age, origin, language, religion, belief, opinion, state of health, disability or any other personal reason without acceptable justification" (unofficial translation).

39. It reads: "Everyone has the freedom of religion and conscience. Freedom of religion and conscience includes the right to profess and practice a religion, the right to express one's convictions and the right to belong or not to belong to a religious community. No one is obliged to engage in the practice of religion against their conscience" (unofficial translation).

40. *Finland 2018 International Religious Freedom Report* (Washington, DC: US Department of State, 2018), 1.

41. It reads: "The buildings used for the public exercise of worship, as well as the movable objects garnishing them, will be left free of charge at the disposal of public establishments of worship" (unofficial translation).

42. "French Islam: Adapting the Law of 1905 to the World of 2018," Government of France, December 10, 2018, accessed April 18, 2020, https://www.gouvernement.fr/en/french-islam-adapting-the-law-of-1905-to-the-world-of-2018.

43. Article 1 reads: "France shall be an indivisible, secular, democratic and social Republic. It shall ensure the equality of all citizens before the law, without distinction of origin, race or religion. It shall respect all beliefs. It shall be ecentral on a ecentralized basis."

44. *France 2018 International Religious Freedom Report* (Washington, DC: US Department of State, 2018), 1.

45. It reads: "(1) Freedom of faith and of conscience and freedom to profess a religious or philosophical creed shall be inviolable. (2) The undisturbed practice of religion shall be guaranteed."

46. *Germany 2018 International Religious Freedom Report* (Washington, DC: US Department of State, 2018), 1.

47. Article 7 reads: "The State and the Catholic Church are independent and sovereign, each within its own sphere."

48. Article 8 reads: "All religious denominations are equally free before the law. Denominations other than Catholicism have the right to self-organisation according to their own statutes, provided these do not conflict with Italian law. Their relations with the State are regulated by law, based on agreements with their respective representatives."

49. *Italy 2018 International Religious Freedom Report* (Washington, DC: US Department of State, 2018), 1.

50. It reads: "Everyone shall have the right to profess freely his religion or belief, either individually or in community with others, without prejudice to his responsibility under the law."

51. *The Netherlands 2018 International Religious Freedom Report* (Washington, DC: US Department of State, 2018), 1.

52. Leyla Yıldırım, "The Social Impact of Islamophobia on Muslims in the Netherlands," *IRCICA Journal Special Issue on Islamophobia in Europe* III, no. 6 (Fall 2015): 155–74.

53. Article 4 reads: "The King shall at all times profess the Evangelical-Lutheran religion."

54. Article 16 reads: "All inhabitants of the realm shall have the right to free exercise of their religion. The Church of Norway, an Evangelical-Lutheran church, will remain the Established Church of Norway and will as such be supported by the State. Detailed provisions as to its system will be laid down by law. All religious and belief communities should be supported on equal terms."

55. "The Constitution of the Kingdom of Norway," Ministry of Justice and Public Security, accessed April 18, 2020, https://lovdata.no/dokument/NLE/lov/1814-05-17?q=grunnloven.

56. "Anders Behring Breivik Had Links to Far-Right EDL, Says Anti-Racism Group," *Guardian*, July 26, 2011.

57. "Norway Hairdresser on Trial for Refusing Client in Hijab," *The Local* (Norway), September 8, 2016.

58. "Norway Hairdresser Fined for Turning Away Client in Hijab," *The Local* (Norway), September 12, 2016.

59. Lucy Pasha-Robinson, "Norwegian Anti-Immigrant Group Mistakes Empty Bus Seats for Women Wearing Burqas," *Independent*, August 1, 2017.

60. Kate Ng, "Norway Terror Suspect 'Regrets' Not Killing More People in Attack on Mosque," *Independent*, May 8, 2020.

61. Freedom House, *Freedom in the World 2020: The Annual Survey of Political Rights and Civil Liberties,* (Lanham, MD: Rowman & Littlefield, 2021), 880.

62. Sindre Bangstad, "Norway is in Denial about the Threat of Far-Right Violence," *Guardian*, September 16, 2019.

63. Article 1(6) of Chapter 2 guarantees "freedom of worship: that is, the freedom to practise one's religion alone or in the company of others."

64. *Sweden 2018 International Religious Freedom Report* (Washington, DC: US Department of State, 2018), 1.

65. Article 15 reads: "1. Freedom of religion and conscience is guaranteed. 2. Every person has the right to choose freely their religion or their philosophical convictions, and to profess them alone or in community with others. 3. Every person has the right to join or to belong to a religious community, and to follow religious teachings. 4. No person may be forced to join or belong to a religious community, to participate in a religious act, or to follow religious teachings."

66. *Switzerland 2018 International Religious Freedom Report* (Washington, DC: US Department of State, 2018), 1.

67. Siobhán O'Grady, "After Refusing A Handshake, A Muslim Couple Was Denied Swiss Citizenship," *Washington Post,* August 18, 2018.

68. It reads: "If a court's determination of any question arising under this Act might affect the exercise by a religious rganization (itself or its members collectively) of the Convention right to freedom of thought, conscience and religion, it must have particular regard to the importance of that right."

69. "Leadership and Governance," The Church of England, accessed April 18, 2020, https://www.churchofengland.org/about/leadership-and-governance.

70. "The Church of Scotland," accessed April 22, 2020, https://www.churchofscotland.org.uk/about-us/our-structure.

71. *United Kingdom 2018 International Religious Freedom Report* (Washington, DC: US Department of State, 2018), 1.

72. Elisa Menendez, "Woman Who 'Choked' Muslim Girl, 14, with Hijab Let Off with Caution," *Metro* (UK), December 10, 2019.

73. Lizzie Dearden, "White Supremacist Behind 'punish a Muslim Day' Jailed for 12 Years," *Independent*, September 3, 2019.

74. Suhaiymah Manzoor-Khan, "Under Boris Johnson, Islamophobia Will Reach a Sinister New Level," *Guardian*, January 5, 2020.

75. "Anti-Muslim Women Remarks: UK PM Refuses to Offer Apology," *The News* (Pakistan), March 12, 2020.

76. "Most Western Europeans Favor at Least Some Restrictions on Muslim Women's Religious Clothing," Pew Research Center, September 17, 2018.

77. Article 2 of the antifacial covering law states: "(1) Anyone who hides or hides his facial features in clothing or other objects in public places or in public

buildings in such a way that they are no longer recognizable, commits an administrative offense and is fined up to 150 euros. The administrative offense can be punished by an administrative fine according to § 50 VStG in the amount of up to 150 euros. Public places or public buildings are places that a group of people who are not restricted from the outset can enter at any time or at certain times, including the non-stationary facilities of public and private bus, rail, air and ship traffic. (2) There is no violation of the ban on covering according to paragraph 1 if the covering or hiding of the facial features is provided for by federal or state law, takes place within the framework of artistic, cultural or traditional events or within the scope of sports or health or professional reasons Has."

78. "Information Leaflet," Federal Ministry of the Interior, accessed April 17, 2020, https://www.bmi.gv.at/bmi_documents/2090.pdf.

79. Chris Baynes, "Austria Burqa Ban: Government Warns Muslim Women to Show Faces in Public or Be Fined," *Independent*, September 22, 2017.

80. Helen Nianias, "Women Forced to Remove the Veil on Day One of Austrian Burqa Ban," *Telegraph*, October 1, 2017.

81. Philip Oltermann, "Austrian Full-Face Veil Ban Condemned as a Failure by Police," *Guardian*, March 27, 2018.

82. "President of the Lawyers against the Burqa Ban," *Wiener Zeitung* (Vienna), September 29, 2017.

83. "Van Der Bellen: Ban on Full Concealment 'Not A Good Law'," *Die Presse* (Vienna), June 8, 2017.

84. Lizzie Dearden, "Austrian President Calls on All Women to Wear Headscarves in Solidarity with Muslims to Fight 'Rampant Islamophobia'," *Independent*, April 28, 2017.

85. Birgit Seiser, "Vienna: Nikab Dispute on the Open Road," *Kurier* (Vienna), October 6, 2017.

86. Philip Oltermann, "Austria Approves Headscarf Ban in Primary Schools," *Guardian*, May 16, 2019.

87. Peter O'Brien, *The Muslim Question in Europe: Political Controversies and Public Philosophies* (Philadelphia: Temple University Press, 2016), 108.

88. Vanessa Mock and John Lichfield, "Belgium Passes Europe's First Ban on Wearing Burka in Public," *Independent,* May 1, 2010.

89. Intissar Kherigi, "A Belgian Face-Veil Ban Would Be Senseless," *Guardian,* April 22, 2010.

90. Alessandro Ferrari and Sabrina Pastorelli, eds., *The Burqa Affair Across Europe: Between Public and Private Space* (New York: Routledge, 2016), 144.

91. Yasmeen Serhan, "Does the Burqa Have a Future in Europe?" *The Atlantic*, July 13, 2017.

92. "Bosnians Protest against Hijab Ban," *Kuwait Times*, February 7, 2016.

93. "Bulgarian Town Bans Face Veil in Public," *Express Tribune* (Pakistan), April 27, 2016.

94. Amnesty International, "Bulgaria: Burqa Ban Part of Disturbing Trend of Intolerance, Xenophobia and Racism," press release, September 30, 2016.

95. Teis Jensen, "Denmark Set to Ban the Burqa despite Fears for Religious Freedom," *Independent*, October 6, 2017.

96. Jørgen Schøler Nielsen, Samim Akgönül, Ahmet Alibašić, Brigitte Maréchal, and Christian Moe, eds., *Yearbook of Muslims in Europe, Volume 1,* (Leiden: Brill, 2009), 455.

97. Elaine Sciolino, "Ban on Head Scarves Takes Effect in France," *New York Times*, September 3, 2004.

98. Elaine Sciolino, "Debate Begins in France on Religion in the Schools," *New York Times*, February 4, 2003.

99. Human Rights Watch, "France: Headscarf Ban Violates Religious Freedom," press release, February 27, 2004.

100. *Annual Report of the United States Commission on International Religious Freedom* (Washington, DC: U.S. Commission on International Religious Freedom, 2004), 53.

101. John R. Bowen, Christophe Bertossi, Jan Willem Duyvendak, and Mona Lena Krook, eds., *European States and their Muslim Citizens* (New York: Cambridge University Press, 2014), 155.

102. Steven Erlanger, "France: Warning Over Veil Ban," *New York Times,* March 30, 2010.

103. Kim Willsher, "France's Burqa Ban Upheld by Human Rights Court," *Guardian,* July 1, 2014.

104. United Nations Human Rights Office of the High Commissioner, "France: Banning the Niqab Violated Two Muslim Women's Freedom of Religion," press release, October 23, 2018.

105. Angelique Chrisafis, "French Mayors Refuse to Lift Burkini Ban despite Court Ruling," *Guardian*, August 28, 2016.

106. Amelia Gentleman, "Row over Headscarves in Schools Reveals Secular Tensions," *Guardian*, September 23, 2003.

107. Human Rights Watch, *Discrimination in the Name of Neutrality: Headscarf Bans for Teachers and Civil Servants in Germany* (New York: HRW, 2009), 58.

108. "Interview by Federal President Johannes Rau with the weekly newspaper Welt am Sonntag," Bundes Praesident, January 4, 2004, accessed April 08, 2020, https://www.bundespraesident.de/SharedDocs/Reden/DE/Johannes-Rau/Interviews/2004/20040104_Rede.html.

109. Federal Constitutional Court, "Order of 27 January 2015: A General Ban on Headscarves for Teachers at State Schools is not Compatible with the Constitution," Press Release No. 14/2015, March 13, 2015.

110. Alison Smale, "Angela Merkel Calls for Ban on Full-Face Veils in Germany," *New York Times*, December 6, 2016.

111. Lizzie Dearden, "German Parliament Votes in Favour of Partial Burqa Ban," *Independent*, April 28, 2017.

112. Lydia Smith, "Drivers Wearing Face Veil in Germany Will Now be Fined as Controversial Ban Comes into Force," *Independent*, September 23, 2017.

113. "Bavaria Pushes Ahead with Burqa Ban as Elections Loom," *Express Tribune* (Karachi), February 22, 2017.

114. "Veil Guidelines at the CAU," Kiel University, February 26, 2019, accessed April 20, 2020, https://www.uni-kiel.de/en/details/news/campus-information-veil.

115. United States Department of State, *Germany: International Religious Freedom Report for 2020* (Washington, DC: Office of International Religious Freedom, 2020), 12.

116. Ashley Cowburn, "Lombardy in Italy Bans Burqas and Islamic Veils Following European Terror Attacks," *Independent*, December 12, 2015.

117. Stephen Schwartz, "Kosovo Says No to the Headscarf in Public Schools," *Washington Examiner*, April 14, 2010.

118. Rachael Pells, "Islamic Face Veil to Be Banned in Latvia Despite Being Worn by Just Three Women in Entire Country," *Independent*, April 21, 2016.

119. "Veil Ban Passed," *Delano News* (Luxembourg), April 27, 2018.

120. Amnesty International, *Report 2013 the State of the World's Human Rights,* (London: Amnesty International, 2013), 182.

121. Daniel Boffey, "Dutch 'burqa ban' Rendered Largely Unworkable on First Day," *Guardian*, August 1, 2019.

122. Jeffrey Haynes, ed., *Routledge Handbook of Religion and Politics* (Oxford: Routledge, 2009), 238.

123. Human Rights Watch, *World Report 2020* (Washington, DC: HRW, 2020), 224.

124. Jon Sharman, "Norway's Parliament Votes to Ban Burqa in Schools and Universities," *Independent*, June 7, 2018.

125. Giles Tremlett, "Burqa Bans Spread across Catalonia," *Guardian*, July 2, 2010.

126. "Swedish Town Bans Islamic Headscarf in Primary Schools," *The Local* (Sweden), May 30, 2019.

127. "Swedish Teachers Don Veils to Support Muslim Students," *Frontier Post* (Peshawar), January 16, 2020.

128. "Swedish Court Finds Ban on Islamic Veil in School Illegal," *The Nation* (Pakistan), June 24, 2021.

129. "Resolution Adopted by the Human Rights Council," UN General Assembly, March 25, 2010.

130. Brian Blackstone, "Swiss Canton Votes to Ban Burqas," *Wall Street Journal*, September 23, 2018.

131. Patrick Wintour, "Minister Gives Schools Right to Ban Muslim Veil," *Guardian*, March 20, 2007.

Chapter Four

The Debate Outside Europe and Muslim Response

UNITED NATIONS ORGANIZATION

The United Nations Plan of Action and Strategy on Hate Speech was announced in May 2019 with a functional definition and clear objectives, but the UN has talked significantly about Islamophobia since 9/11. On January 13, 2004, the UN Secretary General Kofi Annan called for jointly combating "rising" Islamophobia and anti-Semitism. Delivering the inaugural Robert Burns Memorial Lecture at UN headquarters in New York, Mr. Annan criticized those who remained silent in the face of bigotry, saying, "Such passivity must not be allowed to masquerade as tolerance. Many Muslims, particularly in the West, have found themselves the objects of suspicion, harassment, and discrimination."[1] In December 2004, a UN conference tried to find ways to fight Islamophobia. Secretary General Kofi Annan stressed to separate "acts of few extremists" from conduct of all Muslims.[2]

In July 2005, UN Secretary General Kofi Annan established a panel on the Alliance of Civilizations, to submit a report on bridging the gap between different civilizations especially Islam and the West. On February 9, 2006, the deputy director of the UN Office of the Alliance of Civilizations said that controversies like cartoons in Danish newspapers are "an educational issue."[3] On the same day, three UN rights experts made a statement condemning the publication of controversial cartoons in *Jyllands-Posten* as well as subsequent reaction and called for dialogue. Doudou Diene, special rapporteur on contemporary forms of racism, racial discrimination, xenophobia, and related intolerance; , Asma Jahangir, the special rapporteur on freedom of religion or belief; ; and Ambeyi Ligabo, the special rapporteur for the promotion and protection of the right to freedom of opinion and expression, stated that they "strongly deplore the depictions of the Prophet Muhammad and are distressed by the grave offence they have caused to the members of the Muslim community."[4]

On January 30, 2006, Kofi Annan noted corrosion between Islamic and Western cultures seeing it as a danger to global stability.[5] On February 2, 2006, the UN Secretary General expressed his concern over the Danish cartoon controversy and stressed that "free press must respect all religions."[6] The very next day, he urged Muslims to accept *Jyllands-Posten's* apology about controversial cartoons but stated, "I share the distress of the Muslim friends who feel that the cartoon offends their religion. I also respect the right of freedom of speech. But of course, freedom of speech is never absolute. It entails responsibility and judgment."[7]

On February 5, 2006, Annan called for ending the violence that erupted after publication of controversial cartoons.[8] On February 7, 2006, Kofi Annan joined European and Muslim officials to call for a "spirit of friendship and mutual respect." In a joint statement, Kofi Annan, along with the head of the OIC and European Union's senior representative for foreign and security policy, said, "We fully uphold the right of free speech. But we understand the deep hurt and widespread indignation felt in the Muslim World. We believe freedom of the press entails responsibility and discretion and should respect the beliefs and tenets of all religions."[9]

On 9 February, Mr. Annan asked the outlets reprinting controversial cartoons not to "pour oil on the fire." He told reporters at UN headquarters in his most extensive spontaneous comments on the controversy saying, "Honestly, I do not understand why any newspaper will publish the cartoons today, it is insensitive, it is offensive, it is provocative, and they should see what has happened around the world."[10]

On February 20, the UN chief showed his deep concern over the cartoon controversy violence calling to find ways to calm the situation.[11] On April 12, he commented that the caricatures crisis reflected extremism in both Muslim and Western societies that needs to be countered. He told the meeting of the OIC in Istanbul adding that the "rights carry with them an inherent responsibility, and should not be used to degrade, humiliate or insult any group or individual."[12]

In March 2008 when Dutch parliamentarian Geert Wilders released his film, the then UN Secretary General Ban Ki-moon termed that "offensively anti-Islamic" stating that the freedom of expression was not at stake. UN high Commissioner for Human Rights also condemned the "tone and content" of the video while three UN special rapporteurs condemned "distorted vision and irresponsibility" of the film in a joint statement.[13]

UN Secretary General Ban Ki-moon said,

> There is no justification for hate speech or incitement to violence. The right of free expression is not at stake here. I acknowledge the efforts of the Dutch Government to stop the broadcast of this film and appeal for calm to those understandably offended by it. Freedom must always be accompanied by social responsibility.

Doudou Diène, the special rapporteur on contemporary forms of racism, racial discrimination, xenophobia, and related intolerance; Asma Jahangir, the special rapporteur on freedom of religion or belief; and Ambeyi Ligabo, special rapporteur for the promotion and protection of the right to freedom of opinion and expression said in a video that this "illustrates an increasing pattern that associates Muslims exclusively with violence and terrorism."

When *Charlie Hebdo* published controversial cartoons in 2012, the UN human rights chief called the magazine "doubly irresponsible" and lauded efforts of Muslim prominent figures to keep calm amidst protests and killings in the Muslim world. UN High Commissioner for Human Rights Navi Pillay said, "Deliberate and obnoxious acts of this type should be deprived of the oxygen of publicity. Given what happened last week, and the fact that people are being killed, Charlie Hebdo is doubly irresponsible to publish these cartoons."[14]

There was heated debate at the UN in September 2012 when Muslim leaders questioned Western notions of freedom of expression.[15]

When the attacks on *Charlie Hebdo* were carried out in March 2015, UN Secretary General Ban Ki-moon called it a "cold-blooded crime" and an attack on freedom of expression and press. The UN Security Council in New York and United Nations Educational, Scientific and Cultural Organization (UNESCO) in Paris held a moment of silence for the victims of the attacks while the director general of UNESCO strongly condemned the attack in a statement.[16] Ban Ki-moon also offered his condolences to the government of France and termed the attack "criminality."[17] The UN human rights commissioner however warned that the *Charlie Hebdo* attack should not be responded with "discrimination and prejudice" against Muslims. Zeid Ra'ad Al Hussein said that doing so would be playing right into the hands of the terrorists by creating even greater divides between religions and societies: "With xenophobia and anti-migrant sentiments already on the rise in Europe, I am very concerned that this awful, calculated act will be exploited by extremists of all sorts."[18]

In October 2020, the United Nations High Representative for the Alliance of Civilizations stressed for "mutual respect" after reprinting of controversial caricatures.[19]

In March 2021, a report was submitted to the UN Human Rights Council by special rapporteur Ahmed Shaheed warning that hatred against Muslims reaches to "epidemic proportions" along with rampant "negative representations of Islam, hostility, violence and Islamophobia." With reference to European surveys in 2018 and 2019, the report suggests every four out of ten people are against Muslims. The report also accuses states to disproportionately targeting Muslims defining them as high risk. The report points out stereotyping Muslims minorities giving example of "triple penalty" for Muslim women being women, in minority and Muslim. The report highlights reinforcement of such trends by the media, politicians, and cultural and even academic influencers.[20] While addressing an OIC event marking the International Day to Combat Islamophobia, the UN Secretary General mentioned the same report and expressed his concern on this "epidemic of hatred" and "anti-Muslim bigotry."[21]

The issue of defamation of religions has been taken up quite frequently by the UN on various forums. There was a series of resolutions adopted majorly on behalf of the OIC addressing this issue. In December 2002, UNGA adopted resolution 57/208 ("Elimination of All Forms of Religious Intolerance") then in 2003 resolution 58/184, and in 2004 resolution 59/199 with same title was adopted. UNGA resolutions 60/150 (2006), 61/164 (2007), 62/154 (2008), 63/171 (2009), 64/156 (2010), and 65/224 (2011) were passed having the title "Combating Defamation of Religions."

After that, Muslim countries joined hands with Western and other countries to widen the scope of such resolutions and the subsequent resolutions were titled "Combating Intolerance, Negative Stereotyping, Stigmatization, Discrimination, Incitement to Violence and Violence against Persons, Based on Religion or Belief."[22] The Office of the High Commissioner for Human Rights also adopted resolutions 1999/82 on April 30, 1999; 2000/84 on April 26, 2000; 2001/4 on April 18, 2001; 2002/9 on April 15, 2002; 2003/4 on April 14, 2003; and 2004/6 on April 13, 2004 and 2005/3 on April 12, 2005, on "Combating Defamation of Religions."

DEBATE IN HUMAN RIGHTS SPECTRUM: AMNESTY AND HRW

On February 27, 2004, the Human Rights Watch called a ban on wearing religious symbols in state schools a violation of religious freedom and "disproportionately affecting Muslim girls" and said that "the proposed law is an unwarranted infringement on the right to religious practice. For many Muslims, wearing a headscarf is not only about religious expression, it is about religious obligation. The proposed law has raised important issues about religious freedom and the role of the state in France."[23]

On February26, 2009, the Human Rights Watch published a detailed report regarding German headscarf and veil bans titled *Discrimination in the Name of Neutrality* and termed those restrictions "specific" and "discriminating" against Muslims. The report reads:

> Those states that ban religious clothing but still allow Christian symbols explicitly discriminate on the grounds of faith. In any event, in all eight states the ban is applied specifically against Muslim women who wear the headscarf. In practical effect, the ban also discriminates on the grounds of gender. The measures effectively force women to choose between their employment and the manifestation of their religious beliefs, violating their right to freedom of religion and equal treatment. These restrictions have led some women to leave their home state or leave Germany altogether, to prolong maternity and other leave from their employment, or to leave teaching after years of studies and investment in developing their skills. Women concerned feel alienated and excluded, even though many had lived in Germany for decades or even their entire lives or are German-born converts to Islam.[24]

On November 29, 2009, Switzerland prohibited construction of minarets through a popular vote. This vote was called "discriminatory," a "violation of rights," and a result of persisting "anti-Muslim rhetoric" by the Human Rights Watch.[25] Amnesty International had already warned that such action would "breach freedom of religion."[26]

On April 10, 2010, the Belgian lower house of parliament unanimously proposed a ban on identity hiding. Amnesty International called this legislation a "dangerous precedent" and said, "[the ban would] violate the rights to freedom of expression and religion of those women who wear the burqa or niqab as an expression of their identity and beliefs."[27] The Human Rights Watch termed the Belgian ban a violation of rights in a statement: "Bans like this lead to a lose-lose situation. They violate the rights of those who choose to wear the veil and do nothing to help those who are compelled to do so."[28]

On September 15, 2010, France banned face coverings amid criticism from the Human Rights Watch.[29] Amnesty International had demanded that lawmakers should reject such ban.[30]

After the 2015 attacks, France conducted nearly four thousand warrantless raids and four hundred people were put under house arrest from November 2015 to July 2016. The Human Rights Watch called these actions discriminatory that abused "the rights to liberty, privacy and freedom of movement" targeting Muslims in general.[31]

On February 7, 2016, Bosnia and Herzegovina banned religious symbols despite an earlier objection by Amnesty International calling it a "violation of right to freedom of expression and religion."[32]

On August 26, 2016, Amnesty International welcomed the court decision to overturn the so-called burkini ban in France that was "fueling prejudice and intolerance."[33]

On October 1, 2017, Amnesty International termed it a restriction of rights to freedom of expression and religion when Austria placed a ban on face hiding at public places and buildings.[34]

On August 1, 2018, Denmark banned burqas and niqabs on which Amnesty International said this law was Muslim-specific and "neither necessary nor proportionate" and

> will have a particularly negative impact on Muslim women who choose to wear the niqab or burqa. Whilst some specific restrictions on the wearing of full-face veils for the purposes of public safety may be legitimate, this blanket ban is neither necessary nor proportionate and violates the rights to freedom of expression and religion.[35]

Human Rights Watch counted the Danish ban as the "latest in harmful trend" and a "part of a worrisome trend that only marginalizes Muslim women in Europe and penalizes them for expressing their beliefs."[36]

On August 1, 2019, the Netherlands banned face coverings in public places and Amnesty International termed the ban an "infringement of women's right."[37]

THE MUSLIM WORLD

As discussed in the introductory chapter, the following countries have been selected as per their relevance being Muslim majority nations:

Afghanistan: Country's official name is Islamic Republic of Afghanistan having Islam as the state religion under Article 2 of the constitution.[38]

Algeria: Article 2 of the constitution states that "Islam shall be the religion of the State." Article 212(3) specifies that no constitutional amendment can undermine this Article.[39]

Bahrain: "The religion of the State is Islam" under Article 2 of the constitution and Islamic law is the basic source of lawmaking.[40]

Bangladesh: "The state religion of the Republic is Islam" according to Article 2A of the constitution.[41]

Brunei Darussalam: Article 1 of the constitution declares Islam as the official religion.[42]

Egypt: "Islam is the religion of the state" as stated by Article 2 of the constitution having Sharia as the main source of legislation.[43]

Indonesia: Although Islam is not mentioned in the constitution, but Article 29 says that belief in "One and Only God" shall be the basis of the state.[44]
Iran: Article 12 of the constitution recognizes Islam as the official religion with specification of "Twelver Ja'farí school" as the school of law. This provision remains unchangeable.[45]
Iraq: "Islam is the official religion of the State" and lawmaking against Islamic provisions is not allowed as specified by first part of Article 2 of the constitution.[46]
Jordan: "Islam is the religion of the State" as declared by Article 2 of the constitution.[47]
Kuwait: "The state religion is Islam" and Islamic law forms the basis for legislation as mentioned in Article 2 of the constitution.[48]
Libya: Article 1 of the constitution declares Islam to be the religion of the state having Sharia as the main source of lawmaking.[49]
Malaysia: "Islam is the religion of the Federation" according to Article 3 of the constitution.[50]
Maldives: Articles 2 and 10 of the constitution declare Islam to be the state religion and basis of state principles.[51]
Mauritania: Article 1 of the constitution declares the country to be an Islamic republic while Article 5 declares Islam to be the religion of state.[52]
Morocco: "Islam is the religion of the State" as written in Article 3 of the constitution.
Oman: The country is an Islamic state and "the religion of the State is Islam" having Islamic law forming the basis for legislation as specified in Articles 1 and 2, respectively, of the Basic Statute of the State.[53]
Pakistan: "Islam shall be the State religion of Pakistan" according to Article 2 of the constitution while the official name of the country is the Islamic Republic of Pakistan according to Article 1.[54]
Qatar: Islam is the religion of the state and Sharia is the main source of legislation as stipulated by Article 1 of the constitution.[55]
Saudi Arabia: The country is a sovereign Arab Islamic kingdom according to Article 1 of the Basic Law of Government.[56]
Somalia: In the constitution through its Article 2 declares Islam to be the state religion, Sharia to be the basis of lawmaking and prohibition of propagation of any religion other than Islam.[57]
Syria: Although Islam has not been declared the state religion in the constitution, Article 3 states that the president should be Muslim and Islam shall be "a major source of legislation."[58]
Tunisia: Article 1 of the constitution declares Islam to be the religion of state.[59]

Turkey: There is no mentioning of Islam in the constitution, but the country plays a major role in the Muslim world with a heavy Muslim population.
United Arab Emirates: "Islam is the official religion of the Union" as specified by Article 7 of the constitution.[60]
Yemen: The country is an Islamic republic according to Article 1 of the constitution. "Islam is the religion of the state" as mentioned in Article 2 while Article 3 says that all legislation shall be done subject to Islamic Sharia.[61]

THE MUSLIM RESPONSE TO CONTROVERSIES

Muslim response to the major controversies discussed in this research is three-fold:

1. Global or regional level
2. State level
3. Individual level

At all levels, Muslims have condemned the publication and/or broadcasts of controversial material but only a fraction of Islamist groups or individuals resorted to violent means.

At the global or regional level, OIC has set up an Islamophobia observatory that publishes annual reports and monthly bulletins.[62] On July 15, 2011, foreign ministers and high officials of twenty-eight states including the then US secretary of state Hillary Clinton gathered in Istanbul, Turkey, to start the "Istanbul Process." This process aims to implement resolution 16/18 of the UN in letter and spirit that calls for discrimination on basis of religion, etc. Until 2019, seven meetings of the process were held in order to promote dialogue and understanding between the West and the Muslim world on issues like freedom of expression.[63]

At the state level, almost all Muslim countries have spoken against both blasphemous content and violent reaction. Initiatives to promote dialogue have also been taken such as "Dialogue among Civilizations" by the then Iranian president Mohammad Khatami in 2001 after the 9/11 attacks.[64] There have been several calls for dialogue and peaceful engagement with the West by Muslim leaders over the years. Most currently, Prime Minister Imran Khan of Pakistan wrote a letter to the leaders of the Muslim states to unite and break the cycle of hate and extremism. The letter reads:

> The recent statements at the leadership level and incidents of desecration of the Holy Quran are a reflection of this increasing Islamophobia that is spreading in European countries where sizeable Muslim populations reside. I urge all our

> Muslim leaders as a collectivity to raise our voice and explain to the leadership of the non-Muslim, especially Western states, the deep-seated reverence and love all Muslims feel for their divine book, the Holy Quran, and for our Prophet (PBUH). It is time to reach out to 'the other' and end cycles of violence bred of ignorance and hate.[65]

Reactions at all levels to major controversies mentioned above are discussed as under:

Jyllands-Posten Cartoons

Immediately after the publication of cartoons, Muslim reaction started coming in. Eleven ambassadors from Turkey, Saudi Arabia, Iran, Pakistan, Egypt, Indonesia, Algeria, Bosnia and Herzegovina, Libya, Morocco, and the head of the Palestinian General Delegation in Denmark wrote a letter to Prime Minister Anders Fogh Rasmussen on October 12, demanding a meeting with him and urging him "to take all those responsible to task." The OIC also wrote a letter to the Danish prime minister showing concern over the situation.[66]

In response to Muslim ambassadors' letter, on October 21 the Danish prime minister refused to meet with the diplomats and declined the request to act against the paper saying that those who are offended may go to the court against such acts or expressions. The Muslim countries tried to resolve the issue diplomatically having Turkey and Egypt on the front. In November, Turkish prime minister Recep Tayyip Erdoğan arrived in Copenhagen and Egyptian foreign minister along with the Secretary Generals of OIC and Arab League sent letters to the OSCE, OECD, and EU foreign policy coordinator. In solidarity with Danish-Muslim organizations, nearly 3,500 people gathered outside the paper's Copenhagen office on October 14, to protest the publication.[67]

On October 27, a criminal complaint was filed by Danish Muslim groups against the publication of cartoons, but charges were not pressed by a local prosecutor.[68] During December, a coalition of Danish Muslims tried to gather support of Middle Eastern religious and political leaders while visiting the region with their dossier, which was also circulated during a meeting of the OIC in Mecca. On December 6, OIC showed concern at "rising hatred against Islam and Muslims" and using the freedom of expression as a "pretext for defaming religions."[69]

On January 26, Libya announced closure of its embassy in Copenhagen and Saudi Arabia recalled its ambassador from Denmark while demanding an apology and punishment for *Jyllands-Posten*. Several other Muslim countries also expressed concerns. On January 29, the OIC and Arab League demanded a UN resolution condemning the publication of cartoons.[70] After the failure of diplomatic efforts, protests erupted across the Middle East and Muslim-majority countries in late January and were joined by religious and political leaders. Gunmen entered the Gaza offices of the European Union on January 30 demanding an apology from *Jyllands-Posten*, which was tendered the next day followed by a welcome note by Rasmussen.[71]

The protests lasted for months and claimed around two hundred lives[72] while turning violent in different countries. Demonstrators in some cities attacked the Western embassies most prominent of which was the Danish embassy in the Pakistani capital Islamabad, which was bombed on June 2, 2008. The cartoonists had to go into hiding after receiving death threats.

Dutch Film Controversy

There was criticism and protest against the film by Muslims even before its release and thirty ambassadors of Muslim countries met with the Dutch foreign minister on March 7, 2008, to discuss the matter.[73] On March 22, 2008, the antiracism organization Nederland Bekent Kleur (The Netherlands Shows its Colours) organized a protest with substantial Muslim participation against the film.[74] While Muslim leaders in the Netherlands requested fellow Muslims to show restraint and not to attack Dutch interests. Muslims inside and outside the Netherlands reacted to the film calling it blasphemous and Al-Qaeda issued a fatwa to kill Wilders a month prior to release of the film. OIC said the film was to "incite and provoke unrest" and "jeopardize world peace and stability." The Saudi embassy in The Hague termed the film "provocative and full of errors," Iran said it was "heinous, blasphemous and anti-Islamic," and Indonesia regarded it an "insult to Islam hidden under the cover of freedom of expression."[75]

There were protests in almost every Muslim-majority country, but the Dutch foreign affairs minister called to "keep a cool head and warm relations" in an op-ed in the Arabic newspaper *Asharq Al-Awsat* on March 30, 2008.[76] Muslim envoys at the UN Human Rights Council passed a resolution that required an investigation on freedom of opinion and expression to also report "racial or religious discrimination" that abused freedom of expression.[77]

A group of Muslims filed a case against the film *Fitna* and different statements made between 2006 and 2008 by Wilders. He was originally charged in January 2009. The trial began in October 2010 and he was acquitted of all charges on June 23, 2011. Wilders was found guilty of "incitement and encouraging discrimination" by a Dutch court in September 2016 due to his political campaigning against Moroccans. However, he was not given any penalty by the court.[78] In 2018, Wilders announced holding a cartoon contest of drawings of the Prophet Muhammad but cancelled amid protests in the Muslim world and the arrest of a man threatening him to death.[79]

The *Charlie Hebdo* Affair

Around 1.6 million people chanting "I'm Charlie and Muslim" and "Not in the name of Allah" gathered on January 11, 2015, in Paris along with leaders of forty Muslim and non-Muslim countries.[80] On January 14, the magazine again carried a cartoon of the Prophet Muhammad on its cover, which sparked anger among citizens of Muslim countries that resulted in violent protests that included killing of at least ten people and torching forty-five churches in Niger.[81] However, not a single Muslim majority country supported the attack, rather almost all states condemned it. OIC termed the attack against Islamic values. The Muslim media reacted in condemnation of both *Charlie Hebdo* caricatures and killings.[82] Many Muslims condemned the brutal attack but remained unable to support the "I am Charlie" slogan citing their religious emotions as the reason.[83]

When *Charlie Hebdo* reprinted the controversial cartoons in September 2020, Muslim leadership in France said that Muslims should not pay heed to the republishing but rather focus on the trial of the 2015 terror attack.[84] There was strong reaction and protests all over the Muslim world against remarks French president Emmanuel Macron gave after the killing of a teacher in Paris. Turkish president Erdogan said that Macron needs a "mental checkup" while Pakistan's prime minister Imran Khan accused Macron of provocation. There were widespread calls for boycotting French products all over the Muslim world in addition to official condemnation of Macron's remarks by several states. In January 2021, thirty-six nongovernmental organizations from thirteen countries urged the UN Human Rights Council to act against France's "breadth of state abuse against Muslims" citing several actions of French government to systematically sideline Muslims.[85]

WHY MUSLIMS REACT VIOLENTLY?

A major question is: Why do Muslims react violently? Why don't they give equal response utilizing their own right to freedom of expression? This is the most important question and answer "from a Muslim perspective," which encompasses the major essence of our research:

- Europeans and the West, in general, have no religion or set of ideas as important as a religion to be paid back in the same coin.

- Since the majority of the population and leadership of Europe do not practice any religion as such, it is really hard to make them realize the importance of religion in one's life, especially in a Muslim's life.
- Had the majority in Europe had belief in any religion, it is still not permissible for Muslims to attack any other religion or make mockery according to their religion.
- Muslims have an altogether different sense of attachment to their religion and especially their prophet, and it is hard for Europeans to understand and hard for Muslims to make anyone else realize.
- Muslims are ordered by their God to obey and respect every prophet and that is why they cannot utter a single word against holy prophets of any other religion.
- Christians and Jews are called "People of the Book" in the Qur'an with a special status for Muslims, hence it is not possible for a Muslim to question their prophets let alone insult.
- Generally, it has never been a tradition of Muslims to question or insult any other religion or its holy personalities throughout the history.

Muslim conception of freedom of expression and blasphemy is altogether different from that of the West, particularly Europe.

NOTES

1. United Nations, "Annan calls for action to combat rising Islamophobia and anti-Semitism," UN News no. 90922, January 13, 2004.
2. United Nations, "Annan calls for end to negative stereotypes of believers in Islam," UN News no. 122952, December 7, 2004.
3. United Nations, "Education Key to Averting Future 'Cartoon Controversies' – UN Official," UN News no. 168802, February 9, 2006.
4. United Nations, "UN human rights experts call for dialogue in wake of cartoon controversy," UN News no. 168672, February 9, 2006.
5. "Annan Hails Efforts at Intercultural Dialogue during Time of Increasing Intolerance," United Nations press release, January 30, 2006.
6. "On Danish Cartoon Controversy, Annan Says Free Press Must Fully Respect All Religions," United Nations press release, February 2, 2006.
7. "Annan Urges Muslims to Accept Apology about Controversial Danish Cartoon," United Nations press release, February 3, 2006.
8. "Annan Urges End to Violence over Controversial Cartoons," United Nations press release, February 5, 2006.
9. "UN Chief Joins with European and Islamic Officials to Urge Calm on Cartoon Dispute," United Nations press release, February 7, 2006.

10. "Annan Speaks out against Reprinting Controversial Cartoons, Again Condemns Violence," United Nations press release, February 9, 2006.

11. "Concerned over cartoon violence, Annan to attend Qatar intercultural panel," United Nations press release, February 20, 2006.

12. "Addressing Islamic Conference, Annan Urges Efforts to Counter Extremism," United Nations press release, April 12, 2006.

13. "Condemning 'offensively anti-Islamic' Video, Ban Ki-Moon Appeals for Calm," United Nations press release, March 28, 2008.

14. "UN Rights Chief Welcomes Efforts to Restore Calm in Wake of Anti-Islam Film, Cartoons," United Nations press release, September 21, 2012.

15. Paul Richter, "Free speech divides U.N.," *Los Angeles Times*, September 25, 2012.

16. "UN Mourns Slain French Cartoonists," United Nations press release, January 8, 2015.

17. "Ban Offers Condolences to French Government in Wake of 'Charlie Hebdo' Attack," United Nations press release, January 9, 2015.

18. Colum Lynch and Keith Johnson, "Mosque Attacks Spark Fears of Blowback after 'Charlie Hebdo'," Foreign Policy, January 8, 2015.

19. "UN Highlights Mutual Respect as Cartoon Row between Turkey, France Resumes," *Daily Sabah* (Istanbul), October 29, 2020.

20. "Anti-Muslim Hatred Has Reached 'Epidemic Proportions' Says UN Rights Expert, Urging Action by States," United Nations press release, March 4, 2021.

21. "UN Leaders Speak out against Islamophobia and Anti-Muslim Hatred," United Nations press release, March 17, 2021.

22. Jeroen Temperman, *Religious Hatred and International Law: The Prohibition of Incitement to Violence or Discrimination* (Cambridge: Cambridge University Press, 2016), 7.

23. "France: Headscarf Ban Violates Religious Freedom," Human Rights Watch press release, February 27, 2004.

24. "Discrimination in the Name of Neutrality," Human Rights Watch press release, February 26, 2009.

25. "Switzerland: Minaret Ban Violates Rights," Human Rights Watch press release, December 4, 2009.

26. "Switzerland Minaret Ban Would Breach Freedom of Religion Obligations," Amnesty International press release, November 25, 2009.

27. Amnesty International UK, "Belgium veil ban sets dangerous precedent in Europe, says Amnesty," press release, April 30, 2010.

28. "Belgium: Muslim Veil Ban Would Violate Rights," Human Rights Watch press release, April 21, 2010.

29. "France: Face-Veil Ruling Undermines Rights," Human Rights Watch press release, July 3, 2014.

30. "French Politicians Urged to Reject Ban on Full Face Veils," Amnesty International press release, May 19, 2010.

31. "World Report 2017: European Union Events of 2016," Human Rights Watch.

32. "Bosnia and Herzegovina Must Reject Burqa Ban," Amnesty International press release, September 1, 2010.

33. "France: Reaction to Court Decision to Overturn Burkini Ban," Amnesty International press release, August 26, 2016.

34. Amnesty International, *Report 2017/18: The State of The World's Human Rights*, (London: Amnesty International, 2018), 81.

35. "Denmark Becomes Latest European Country to Ban Burqas and Niqabs," *Independent*, May 31, 2018.

36. Hillary Margolis, "Denmark's Face Veil Ban Latest in Harmful Trend," Human Rights Watch press release, June 1, 2018.

37. Daniel Boffey, "Dutch 'burqa ban' Rendered Largely Unworkable on First Day," *Guardian*, August 1, 2019.

38. Article 2 reads: The sacred religion of Islam is the religion of the Islamic Republic of Afghanistan. Followers of other faiths shall be free within the bounds of law in the exercise and performance of their religious rituals.

39. Article 212(3) reads: No constitutional amendment shall undermine: 3. Islam as the religion of the State.

40. Article 2 reads: The religion of the State is Islam. The Islamic Shari'a is a principal source for legislation. The official language is Arabic.

41. Article 2A reads: The state religion of the Republic is Islam, but the State shall ensure equal status and equal right in the practice of the Hindu, Buddhist, Christian and other religions.

42. Part of Article 1 reads: The official religion of Brunei Darussalam shall be the Islamic Religion.

43. Article 2 reads: Islam is the religion of the state and Arabic its official language. Principles of Islamic Sharia are the principal source of legislation.

44. Article 29(1) reads: The State shall be based upon the belief in the One and Only God.

45. Article 12 reads: The official religion of Iran is Islam and the madhhab (school of law) is the Twelver Ja'farí school, and this article will remain forever unalterable.

46. First part of Article 2 reads: Islam is the official religion of the State and is a foundation source of legislation: A. No law may be enacted that contradicts the established provisions of Islam.

47. Article 2 reads: Islam is the religion of the State and Arabic is its official language.

48. Article 2 reads (translated online): The state religion is Islam, and Islamic law is a main source of legislation.

49. Part of Article 1 reads: Islam shall be its religion and Islamic Shari'a shall be the main source of legislation.

50. Article 3(1) reads: Islam is the religion of the Federation; but other religions may be racticed in peace and harmony in any part of the Federation.

51. Article 10 reads: (a) The religion of the State of the Maldives is Islam. Islam shall be the one of the bases of all the laws of the Maldives (b) No law contrary to any tenet of Islam shall be enacted in the Maldives. Article 2 reads: The Maldives is a sovereign, independent, democratic Republic based on the principles of Islam.

52. Article 1 reads: Mauritania is an Islamic, indivisible, democratic, and social Republic. Article 5 reads: Islam is the religion of the people and of the State.

53. Article 1 reads: The Sultanate of Oman is an Arab, Islamic, Independent State with full sovereignty and Muscat is its Capital. Article 2 reads: The religion of the State is Islam and Islamic Sharia is the basis for legislation.

54. Article 1(1) reads: Pakistan shall be Federal Republic to be known as the Islamic Republic of Pakistan.

55. Part of Article 1 reads: Qatar is an independent sovereign Arab State. Its religion is Islam and Shari'a law shall be a main source of its legislations.

56. Article 1 reads: The Kingdom of Saudi Arabia is a sovereign Arab Islamic State. Its religion is Islam. Its constitution is Almighty God's Book, The Holy Quran, and the Sunna (Tradition) of the Prophet (PBUH).

57. Article 2 reads: 1. Islam is the religion of the State. 2. No religion other than Islam can be propagated in the country. 3. No law which is not compliant with the general principles of Shari'ah can be enacted.

58. Part of Article 3 reads: The religion of the President of the Republic is Islam; Islamic jurisprudence shall be a major source of legislation.

59. Article 1 reads: Tunisia is a free, independent, sovereign state; its religion is Islam, its language Arabic, and its system is republican. This article might not be amended.

60. Article 7 reads: Islam is the official religion of the Union. The Islamic Shari'ah shall be a main source of legislation in the Union. The official language of the Union is Arabic.

61. Part of Article 1 reads: The Republic of Yemen is an Arab, Islamic and independent sovereign state. Article 2 reads: Islam is the religion of the state, and Arabic is its official Language. Article 3 reads: Islamic Shari'ah is the source of all legislation.

62. "Islamophobia," OIC, accessed April 4, 2021, https://www.oic-oci.org/page/?p_id=182&p_ref=61&lan=en.

63. "Istanbul Process," Istanbul Process, accessed April 4, 2021, https://www.istanbulprocess1618.info/16-18-process/.

64. "Dialogue Among Civilizations: Contexts and Perspectives," United Nations press release.

65. "'Time to Reach out to the other': PM Imran Urges Muslim Leaders to Take a Stand against Rising Islamophobia," *Dawn* (Karachi), October 28, 2020.

66. Nanna Hvidt and Hans Mouritzen, eds., *Danish Foreign Policy Yearbook 2007* (Copenhagen, Danish Institute for International Studies, 2007), 54.

67. Jytte Klausen, *The Cartoons That Shook the World* (New Haven, CT: Yale University Press, 2009), 186, 63–83.

68. "Decision on Possible Criminal Proceedings in the Case of Jyllands-Posten's Article 'The Face of Muhammed'," Director of Public Prosecutions, File No. RA-2006-41-0151, March 15, 2006.

69. Daniel Howden, David Hardaker, and Stephen Castle, "How a Meeting of Leaders in Mecca Set off the Cartoon Wars around the World," *Independent*, February 10, 2006.

70. "Muslims seek UN action on blasphemous cartoons: Libya closes embassy in Denmark," *Dawn* (Karachi), January 30, 2006.

71. Nicholas Watt, "Danish Paper Sorry for Muhammad Cartoons," *Guardian*, January 31, 2006.

72. Jérôme Lambert and Philippe Picard, "Charlie Hebdo, Before the Massacre," *New York Times*, January 9, 2015.

73. "The Netherlands: Concern Over Film," *New York Times*, March 6, 2008.

74. "Dutch Protest Against Islam Critics," *Dawn* (Karachi), March 23, 2008.

75. Niclas Mika, "Muslim Nations Condemn Dutch Qur'an Film," *Mail & Guardian* (Johannesburg), March 29, 2008.

76. "Verhagen: Keep Your Head Cool and Relations Warm," *Eindhovens Dagblad*, March 30, 2008.

77. "Arabs, Muslims Battle US, Europeans over Free Speech at UN," *Daily News Egypt*, April 4, 2008.

78. Gordon Darroch, "Geert Wilders Found Guilty of Inciting Discrimination," *Guardian*, December 9, 2016.

79. Samuel Osbourne, "Dutch Anti-Islam Politician Geert Wilders Cancels Prophet Muhammad Cartoon Competition," *Independent*, August 31, 2018.

80. Liz Alderman and Dan Bilefsky, "Huge Show of Solidarity in Paris against Terrorism," *New York Times*, January 11, 2015.

81. "Anti-Charlie Hebdo Protest: 10 Killed, 45 Churches Set on Fire in Niger," *Tribune India*, January 20, 2015.

82. "The Muslim World Expresses Solidarity in the Aftermath of the Paris Shooting," Middle East Policy Council, accessed April 20, 2020, https://mepc.org/commentary/muslim-world-expresses-solidarity-aftermath-paris-shooting.

83. Clarence Page, "Sorry, I am not 'Charlie'," *Chicago Tribune*, January 10, 2015.

84. Norimitsu Onishi, "Charlie Hebdo Republishes Cartoons That Prompted Deadly 2015 Attack," *New York Times*, September 1, 2020.

85. "Civil Society Groups from 13 Countries Call on UN to Address France's Anti-Islam Actions," *Daily Sabah* (Istanbul), January 18, 2021.

Chapter Five

Freedom of Expression and Religion in the Muslim World

HUMAN FREEDOM AND DIGNITY IN ISLAM

Humans have been given special status in Islam and the same has been mentioned several times in the Qur'an.[1] According to the Qur'an, humans are the most favorite and chosen creature of Allah before whom angels prostrated.[2] The Qur'an says that the God honored Children of Adam[3] against all creatures and designated humans as the caliph of Allah on earth[4] to represent Him as viceroy. Allah also says that He created humans as His best creature[5] and everything on the earth is produced for humans[6] being at their disposal.[7] Human life is therefore much precious and taking one's life unjustly is tantamount to killing whole humanity and saving one life means saving all human beings.[8] The Qur'an declares that all human beings are equal and the only cause of preference could be piety.[9] The Prophet Muhammad also declared the same in his last sermon[10] in addition to other narrations.

FREEDOM OF EXPRESSION IN ISLAM

The Qur'an establishes certain benchmarks for speech and expression. Sura 2 mentions a covenant of Allah with the Children of Israel to *speak kindly to people*.[11] Another verse of the same sura prohibits to *mix truth and false* alike and to *conceal the truth*.[12]

It is ordered in sura 31 to *subdue the voice* and be *modest* while talking to people.[13] There are strong verses in sura 49 regarding *ridiculing* someone, calling with bad *nicknames*, investigation of *false news*, *backbiting*, and *suspicion*. It is ordered to investigate any news before taking an action against anyone on the basis of that that is, spreading false news and accepting that without thorough probe is forbidden.[14]

It is ordered not to *deride*, *defame*, and/or *insult* someone with bad nicknames.[15] Over-suspicion, spying, and especially backbiting is strictly prohibited as well.[16] In another chapter, *slander* and *traduce* are also strictly forbidden.[17] It is ordered to call toward Allah with *wisdom and fair expression* and to have a debate with opposers with good reasoning and *best possible manner*.[18] The same is emphasized more in the case of Abrahamic religions and Muslims are instructed to *argue* with followers of divine scriptures in a way that is *most suitable*.[19] The Qur'an discourages negative *quarrel* and *useless debate* while ordering the followers to avoid those who try to engage you in meaningless argument with ill-intention.[20] It is also commended to *shun the lie*[21] and always utter words that are directed toward *right direction* without any dual meaning.[22] It is not allowed for Muslims to *insult others' gods*[23] and this is one of the fundamental principles of Islam regarding freedom of expression and its limitations in terms of religion. *Slander* and *scandalization* are again condemned[24] in the Qur'an and it is also stressed not to utter *harsh speech* or disclose anyone's *secrets* except where necessary.[25]

The teachings of the Prophet Muhammad also specify certain guidelines for Muslims in connection to the freedom of expression and its limitations. In one narration, the Prophet is reported to have said that *concealing the weaknesses*[26] of a fellow by Muslims is a big deed. The Prophet also instructed Muslims not to reveal *secret*[27] of anyone and the conduct of His companions was accordingly. Violating *privacy*[28] of anyone is a serious crime according to one saying of the Prophet. Listening *secretly*[29] to any other being is also strictly prohibited and *keeping secret*[30] is a religious duty of every Muslim. In another Hadith, the Prophet Muhammad said, "A *Qattaat*[31] will not enter paradise." Attributing false information to someone is severely condemned both in the form of *slander and backbiting*.[32] A Muslim is not permitted to *humiliate* and *look down upon* his fellow and to violate his *honor*.[33]

FREEDOM OF RELIGION IN ISLAM

It is made clear in the Qur'an that "there is no compulsion in religion," that is, the most righteous among religions is clear and the most righteous path within the religion of Islam is also clear so no one should be compelled to follow a particular path rather they should decide without any compulsion.[34] The Qur'an seeks its followers to believe in all prophets and not to distinguish among them.[35] It is ordered to show kindness and deal justly with the non-Muslims who have not fought and driven Muslims out of their homes.[36]

The Qur'an also declares that it has separated truth from false and it is now everyone's prerogative to adopt whatever they wish.[37] Choice is given to everyone to accept or reject the message of the Qur'an – stating that whoever accepts will be having advantage.[38] It is repeatedly stated in the Qur'an that the Prophet Muhammad had no duty to make everyone believe, he was just a messenger.[39] In another sura, the Prophet Muhammad is directed to tell nonbelievers that their religion is for them and my religion is for me.[40] "The Medina Document" regards Jews and Muslims a single community (Ummah)[41] being followers of their respective religions.[42]

FREEDOM OF EXPRESSION, RELIGION, AND BLASPHEMY LAWS IN THE MUSLIM WORLD

In the Muslim world, different countries have different constitutional and legal injunctions protecting the right to freedom of expression and religion. Blasphemy and apostasy laws are continuously debated in different schools of thought within the Islamic world. A general understanding is based on a few verses of the Qur'an and narrations of the Prophet Muhammad. A widely quoted verse in this regard talks about punishment for the apostate in the hereafter.[43] Another verse declares that Allah will never forgive the persons who believe and then disbelieve.[44]

A few sayings of the Prophet Muhammad are also referred to in order to establish that he authorized killing of an apostate.[45] Basic relation of apostasy and its punishment to blasphemy is that insulting Allah and the Prophet Muhammad is equivalent to apostasy and to favor this, companion of the Prophet Muhammad Ibn Abbas is frequently quoted as saying the same.[46] Similar argument has been adopted by a majority of scholars throughout Islamic history to declare that any blaspheme should be punished to death. Many Muslim countries devised their constitutions and penal laws accordingly.

Below is a country-wise discussion of laws regulating freedom of expression and religion as well as blasphemy and apostasy in different states, especially Muslim majority countries:

Afghanistan: The constitution of Afghanistan through its Article 34 declares that the right to freedom of expression is "inviolable" for every Afghan citizen.[47] Articles 347 and 348 in chapter 18 of the Afghan penal code prohibit stopping rituals and rites of any religion; destroying or damaging any religious places, signs, or symbols and publicly attacking a follower of any religion by word, act, writing, or other public means.[48] There is no specific provision to punish blasphemy in the Afghan constitution or penal code.

Figure 5.1. Apostacy laws (2014).

Source: Theodorou, Angelina E., "Apostasy laws, 2014" Pew Research Center, Washington, D.C. (July 29, 2016) http://assets.pewresearch.org/wpcontent/uploads/sites/12/2016/07/FT_16.08.01_restrictions_apostasy640px.png

Figure 5.2. Blasphemy laws (2014).

Source: Theodorou, Angelina E., "Apostasy laws, 2014" Pew Research Center, Washington, D.C. (July 29, 2016)

But the penal code in Article 1 states that crimes of *Hudood, Qisaas*, or *Diat* are to be dealt with according to the Islamic (Hanafi) jurisprudence.[49]

Algeria: Freedom of expression, association, and assembly are guaranteed by Article 48 of the constitution. Article 50 guarantees freedom of the press unless it affects dignity, liberty, and the rights of others.[50] Article 42 of the constitution declares freedom of conscience and freedom of opinion as "inviolable" and guarantees freedom of worship under the law. Article 144(2)[51] of the Algerian penal code penalizes offending the Prophet Muhammad and other prophets and messengers of God with imprisonment of three to five years and/or fines of 50,000 to 100,000 Algerian dinars. Article 160[52] talks about imprisonment from five to ten years of anyone who damages the sacred book.[53] The Information Code regulating media through its Article 26[54] forbids any publication against Islamic morals[55] and through Article 77[56] bans insult to Islam, Christianity, and Judaism.[57]

Bahrain: Freedom of opinion and expression is guaranteed by Article 23 of the constitution with certain limitations including no infringement of Islamic doctrine.[58] Article 22 of the constitution guarantees freedom of conscience and inviolability of practicing any religion.[59] Article 311[60] of the Bahrain penal code also talks about punishments to anyone who obstructs freedom of religion.[61] Article 309[62] of the Bahrain penal code prohibits offending any religious sect with punishment of up to one year or a fine not exceeding 100 Bahraini dinar. Same punishments can be given under Article 310[63] to anyone who deliberately alters a holy book or insults any religious symbol, ceremony, ritual, etc.[64]

Bangladesh: Freedom of thought, conscience, and speech are protected by Article 39 of the constitution subject to any "reasonable restrictions" under the law.[65] Right is given to every citizen for professing, practicing, or propagating their religion under Article 41 provided "law, public order and morality" are not affected.[66] Article 295A[67] of the penal code bars everyone from deliberately and maliciously outraging and insulting religious feelings of any citizen. Deliberately wounding religious feelings is also prohibited under Article 298[68] of the same code. Both crimes are punishable with imprisonment and/or fine.[69]

Brunei Darussalam: There is no specific mentioning of freedom of expression in the constitution. Article 1 of the constitution states that all religions may be practiced with harmony.[70] A new Islamic penal code enacted in 2013 mentions severe punishments for apostasy and blasphemy. Articles 108[71] and 109[72] punish any person who declares themself as God and prophet. Contempt of prophet is punishable under Article 110[73] while Article 111[74] criminalizes deriding the Qur'an, Hadith, or Islamic decided matters. Article 112[75] makes it punishable to declare themself as non-Muslim for any Muslim.[76]

Egypt: "Freedom of thought and opinion" by any means of expression is given to every citizen by Article 45 of the constitution.[77] Freedom of belief is deemed an "inviolable" right under Article 43 of the constitution.[78] Insulting or abusing any religious messenger and prophet is forbidden under Article 44[79] of the constitution.[80] Penalty of detention or paying fine shall be inflicted upon a person insulting any heavenly religion, national unity, or social peace under Article 98F[81] of the Egyptian Criminal Code.[82] Also, articles 160, 161, 176, and 178 of the same code prohibit various forms religious blasphemy.

Indonesia: Freedom to express opinion by means of writing and speaking is protected and regulated by law according to Article 28 of the constitution.[83] Articles 28 and 29 in the constitution give complete liberty of choosing and practicing any religion to every citizen.[84] It is a crime under Article 156(a)[85] of the penal code to abuse any religion and to prevent a person to adhere to any religion that recognizes the almighty God.[86]

Iran: Article 24 of the constitution grants freedom of expression to publications and the press provided it is not detrimental to fundamentals of Islam and public rights. Article 175 gives freedom to express and disseminate ideas through radio and television in line with norms of Islam and national interest.[87] Article 14 quotes a verse from the Qur'an and in light of that declares this a duty of the government and Muslim citizens to treat non-Muslims with respect according to Islamic and ethical principles provided they are not engaged in "conspiracy and hostile measures against Islam" and the state.[88] Article 513[89] of the Islamic Penal Code talks about execution of anyone who insults the Prophet Muhammad and imprisonment from one to five years for anyone who insults sacred values of Islam, great prophets, Shiite imams and holy Fatima. Insulting the founder of the Islamic republic and/or supreme leader is punishable with imprisonment for six months to two years according to Article 214[90] of the penal code.[91] Press Law of 1986 restricts the print media not to violate "Islamic principles and codes as well as public rights." Article 26[92] of the same law says anyone insulting Islam to the extent of apostacy shall be sentenced as an apostate or according to the Islamic Penal Code if not declared an apostate.[93]

Iraq: Article 38 of the constitution binds the state to guarantee freedom of expression by all means provided public order and morality are not violated.[94] The second part of Article 2 in the constitution assures "freedom of religious belief and practice" to all citizens especially minorities. Freedom of religion is also given to all Iraqis by Article 41 and 42 of the constitution.[95] Section two in chapter 8 of the penal code protects minorities through its paragraph 372[96] against attack, disruption, insult and imitation, etc. There is no provision relating to the majority religion, that is, Islam whatsoever.[97]

Jordan: Freedom of opinion and expression is granted by Article 15 of the constitution provided the law is not violated.[98] Article 14 of the constitution grants religious freedom to everyone consistent with public order or morality.[99] Publicly offending any prophet is a crime under Article 273[100] of the penal code while Article 278[101] criminalizes any published material or speech offensive to anyone's religious feelings.[102] Article 5[103] of the Press and Publications Law restricts any publication harming freedom, human rights, and Islamic values.[104]

Kuwait: Article 36 of the constitution guarantees freedom of opinion and right to express that according to law.[105] Freedom of belief is regarded "absolute" under Article 35 of the constitution. Everyone is free to practice religion provided public order and morals are not violated.[106] "Ridicule, contempt or reduction of religion" is forbidden under Article 111[107] of the penal code with a fine or term in prison.[108] Newspapers are not allowed to meddle, defame, slander, or mock the God, prophets, the Qur'an, and companions and family of the Prophet Muhammad under Article 19[109] of the law on press and publications.[110]

Libya: Freedom of opinion and expression is enshrined in Article 14 of the constitution through all means.[111] State guarantees freedom of religion to non-Muslims through Article 1 of the constitution.[112] Publicly attacking Islam and insulting God and prophets is punishable with a detention up to two years in prison according to Article 291[113] of the penal code. Punishment of imprisonment not exceeding one year or a fine up to 50 Libyan dollars shall be given to anyone who interferes with religious rites and damages religious sites under Article 289[114] and same shall apply if any holy book is altered or any religious ceremony is ridiculed under Article 290[115] of the penal code.[116]

Malaysia: In the constitution, Article 10a gives everyone the "right to freedom of speech and expression."[117] The "right to profess and practice" any religion is guaranteed by Article 11 of the constitution. However, propagation of any other religion among Muslims is restricted under clause 4 of the same Article.[118] Insulting any religion, defiling the Qur'an, wounding the religious feelings of anyone, and causing disharmony on religious grounds is punishable under Sections 295[119] and 298[120] of the penal code.[121]

Maldives: Freedom of thought, communication, and opinion is granted by Article 27 of the constitution.[122] Section 617[123] of the criminal code declares it to be class 1 offense to criticize Islam by various means.[124]

Mauritania: Through Article 10 of its constitution gives every citizen freedom of expression, thought, and opinion.[125] Insulting Islam and apostasy is punishable with imprisonment, fine, and death, respectively, under Article 306[126] of the penal code.[127]

Morocco: Articles 25 and 28 of the constitution talk about freedom of expression and the press.[128] Freedom of religion is ensured by Article 3 of the constitution.[129] Article 220[130] of the penal code criminalizes preventing practice of any cult and shaking faith of a Muslim with imprisonment and fine.[131]

Oman: In the Basic Statute of the State, Article 29 ensures freedom of opinion and expression through all means.[132] Freedom to practice religion is protected by Article 28 of the basic statute provided public order is not disturbed and morals are not contradicted.[133] Insulting the divine, the Qur'an, Islam, or any Abrahamic religion and its buildings and any prophet is punishable by term in jail between three and ten years as mentioned in Article 269[134] of the penal law. Articles 270, 271, and 272 forbid disparaging pillars of Islam by various means while Article 273[135] mentions punishment of imprisonment between ten days to a year or fine between one hundred to one thousand Omani rial for offending Islam or any Abrahamic religion.[136]

Pakistan: Article 19 of the constitution entitles every citizen to the right to freedom of speech and expression with certain restrictions relating to Islam, national security, foreign relations, public order, decency or morality, contempt of court, and incitement to offence.[137] Right to "profess, practice and propagate" any religion is granted to every national by Article 20 of the constitution "subject to law, public order and morality."[138] Chapter XV of the Pakistan Penal Code deals with the offenses relating to religion. Section 295[139] and 295A[140] punish damaging places of worship and insulting any religion with a term in jail or fine or both. Imprisonment for life is described as punishment for anyone who defiles the Qur'an in Section 295B[141] and death punishment or imprisonment for life with fine is detailed in Section 295C[142] for insulting the Prophet Muhammad. Wounding anyone's religious feelings is liable to a term in jail of up to one year, or fine, or both under Section 298.[143] Insulting the family, successors, and companions of the Prophet Muhammad is a crime under Section 298A[144] with punishment of up to three years in prison, or fine, or both. Sections 298B and C restrict Qadianis from calling themselves Muslims, preach or propagate their faith, and adopt Islamic titles etc.[145]

Qatar: Article 47 of the constitution promises freedom of expression of opinion in accordance with the law.[146] Article 50 of the constitution stipulates that freedom to practice religion is the right of every citizen provided public order and morality are observed.[147] Article 1[148] of the penal code specifies that crimes concerning Muslims including apostasy shall be dealt with in accordance with Islamic Sharia. Article 256[149] mentions conviction of up to seven years in jail for offending the Qur'an, Islamic rites, divine religions, and prophets, etc. Articles 257 to 262 declare it a crime to oppose and/or challenge basic tenets of Islam by various means and Article 263[150] prohibits offending Islam or Abrahamic religions.[151]

Saudi Arabia: All means of expression are bound under Article 39 of the Basic Law of Government to employ civil and polite language and shall not harm human dignity, security, and public relations of the state.[152] The Basic Law does not explicitly mention religious freedom but Article 26 protects "human rights in accordance with Sharia."[153] There are no specific blasphemy laws but Article 48 of the Basic Law leaves it to the courts to work in accordance with Islamic law in every respect.[154]

Somalia: Through Article 18 of its constitution grants freedom of expression and opinion.[155] Article 17 of the constitution promises freedom of religion without permission of propagating any religion other than Islam.[156] Penal code through its Articles 313 and 314[157] suggests imprisonment for anyone who insults Islam and/or disturbs its observance.[158]

Syria: Freedom of opinion and expression is granted by Article 42 of the constitution.[159] Protection to freedom of belief is provided in accordance with the law under Article 42 of the constitution.[160] Article 208 of the penal code describes public venue and Article 462,[161] 463, and 464 prohibit disparaging religious rituals by various means.[162]

Tunisia: Right to freedom of creative freedom and audiovisual expression is guaranteed by Articles 42 and 127, respectively, of the constitution while freedom of expression is protected by Article 31.[163] Article 6 of the constitution declares that the state is the guardian of religion and protects freedom of conscience and belief.[164] The country's penal code does not specify religious blasphemy but its Article 121bis[165] criminalizes distribution and propagation of prohibited material that can cause harm to public order and/or morals. Undermining good morals by any means is also punishable under Article 226bis[166] of the penal code.[167]

Turkey: The constitution grants freedom of thought and opinion to everyone through its Article 25 while Article 26 gives freedom to express and disseminate thoughts with certain legal limitations not related to religion.[168] Article 24 of the constitution guarantees freedom of religion and conscience to everyone.[169] There is no blasphemy law as such but Article 24 of the constitution prohibits exploiting or abusing religion or religious feelings.[170] Sections 1 and 2 of the penal code generally criminalize hatred, hostility, and degradation but Section 3[171] specifically talks about degrading religious values with imprisonment of six months to one year.[172]

United Arab Emirates: Article 30 of the constitution guarantees freedom of opinion and expression by all means "within the limits of law."[173] "Freedom to exercise religious worship" is given to every citizen by Article 32 of the constitution subject to public policy and morals.[174] Offense against Islam and any other recognized religion is punishable under Article 312[175] of the penal code with minimum confinement of one year or fine.[176]

Yemen: Article 42 of the constitution guards the right to freedom of expression by various means "within the limits of law."[177] The constitution does not mention freedom of religion in particular. Article 60 of the constitution declares it a national duty to defend religion and the homeland.[178] Contempt of religion in general is forbidden by Article 194[179] of the penal code with no more than three years in prison or fine but if the affected religion is Islam, then the term in jail shall be up to five years or a fine as Article 195[180] further specifies. Article 259[181] of the same code mentions the death penalty for apostasy, Article 260[182] states that distorting the Qur'an shall be punishable by five years in jail or fine, and Article 261[183] punishes anyone committing assault on religion with a maximum of one year in prison or a fine not more than two thousand riyals.[184]

NOTES

1. All translations are taken from Mohammed Marmaduke Pickthall, trans., *The Meaning of the Glorious Quran* (New York: Alfred A. Knopf, 1930).
2. Al-Hijr 15, Verses 28–30 read: And (remember) when thy Lord said unto the angels: Lo! I am creating a mortal out of potter's clay of black mud altered. So, when I have made him and have breathed into him of My Spirit, do ye fall down, prostrating yourselves unto him. So the angels fell prostrate, all of them together.
3. Bani Israel 17, Verse 70 reads: Verily We have honoured the Children of Adam.
4. Al-Baqarah 2, Verse 30 reads: And when thy Lord said unto the angels: Lo! I am about to place a viceroy in the earth.
5. At-Tin 95, Verse 4 reads: Surely We created man of the best stature.
6. Al-Baqarah, Verse 29 reads: He it is Who created for you all that is in the earth.
7. Luqmaan 31, Verse 20 reads: See ye not how Allah hath made serviceable unto you whatsoever is in the skies and whatsoever is in the earth.
8. Al-Ma'idah 5, Verse 32 reads: Whosoever killeth a human being for other than manslaughter or corruption in the earth, it shall be as if he had killed all mankind, and whoso saveth the life of one, it shall be as if he had saved the life of all mankind.
9. Al-Hujuraat 49, Verse 13 reads: O mankind! Lo! We have created you male and female, and have made you nations and tribes that ye may know one another. Lo! The noblest of you, in the sight of Allah, is the best in conduct. Lo! Allah is Knower, Aware.
10. All mankind is from Adam and Eve. An Arab has no superiority over a non-Arab, nor does a non-Arab have any superiority over an Arab; white has no superior-

ity over black, nor does a black have any superiority over white; [none have superiority over another] except by piety and good action.

11. Al-Baqarah, Verse 83 reads: And speak kindly to mankind.

12. Ibid. Verse 42 reads: Confound not truth with falsehood, nor knowingly conceal the truth.

13. Luqmaan, Verse 19 reads: Be modest in thy bearing and subdue thy voice.

14. Al-Hujuraat, Verse 6 reads: O ye who believe! If an evil-liver bring you tidings, verify it, lest ye smite some folk in ignorance and afterward repent of what ye did.

15. Ibid. Verse 11 reads: O ye who believe! Let not a folk deride a folk who may be better than they (are), nor let women (deride) women who may be better than they are; neither defame one another., nor insult one another by nicknames. Bad is the name of lewdness after faith. And whoso turneth not in repentance, such are evil-doers.

16. Ibid. Verse 12 reads: O ye who believe! Shun much suspicion; for lo! Some suspicion is a crime. And spy not, neither backbite one another. Would one of you love to eat the flesh of his dead brother? Ye abhor that (so abhor the other)! And keep your duty (to Allah). Lo! Allah is Relenting, Merciful.

17. Al-Humazah 104, Verse 1 reads: Woe unto every slandering traducer.

18. Al-Nahl 16, Verse 125 reads: Call unto the way of thy Lord with wisdom and fair exhortation, and reason with them in the better way. Lo! Thy Lord is best aware of him who strayeth from His way, and He is Best Aware of those who go aright.

19. Al-Ankabut 29, Verse 46 reads: And argue not with the People of the Scripture unless it be in (a way) that is better.

20. Al-Furqaan 25, Verse 63 reads: The (faithful) slaves of the Beneficent are they who walk upon the earth modestly, and when the foolish ones address them answer: Peace.

21. Al-Hajj 22, Verse 30 reads: And shun lying speech.

22. Al-Ahzaab 33, Verse 70 reads: O ye who believe! Guard your duty to Allah, and speak words straight to the point.

23. Al-Anaam 6, Verse 109 reads: Revile not those unto whom they pray beside Allah Jest they wrongfully revile Allah through ignorance. Thus, unto every nation have We made their deed seem fair. Then unto their Lord is their return and He will tell them what they used to do.

24. An-Noor 24, Verse 19 reads: Lo! Those who love that slander should be spread concerning those who believe, theirs will be a painful punishment in the world and the Hereafter. Allah knoweth. Ye know not.

25. An-Nisa 4, Verse 148 reads: Allah loveth not the utterance of harsh speech save by one who hath been wronged. Allah is ever Hearer, knower.

26. Part of Hadith 2699a in Sahih Al-Muslim reads: He who conceals (the faults) of a Muslim, Allah would conceal his faults in the world and in the Hereafter.

27. Hadith 2482b in Sahih Al-Muslim reads: Anas b. Malik reported that Allah's Apostle told me something secretly. I informed none about that and Umm Sulaim asked me about it, but I did not tell her even.

28. Hadith 2158a in Sahih Al-Muslim reads: He who peeped into the house of people without their consent, it is permissible for them to put out his eyes.

29. Part of Hadith 7042 in Sahih Al-Bukhari reads: If somebody listens to the talk of some people who do not like him (to listen) or they run away from him, then molten lead will be poured into his ears on the Day of Resurrection.

30. Hadith 1959 in Jami At-Tirmidhi reads: When a man narrates a narration, then he looks around, then it is a trust.

31. Hadith 6056 in Sahih Al-Bukhari: *Qattaat* is a person who conveys disagreeable, false information from one person to another with the intention of causing harm and enmity between them. [Definition from: Muhammad Muhsin Khan, trans., *Sahih Al-Bukhari* (Riyadh: Darussalam, 1997), 8:55.]

32. Hadith 2589 in Sahih Al-Muslim reads: Abu Huraira reported Allah's Messenger (ﷺ) as saying: Do you know what is backbiting? They (the Companions) said: Allah and His Messenger know best. Thereupon he (the Holy Prophet) said: Backbiting implies your talking about your brother in a manner which he does not like. It was said to him: What is your opinion about this that if I actually find (that failing) in my brother which I made a mention of? He said: If (that failing) is actually found (in him) what you assert, you in fact backbited him, and if that is not in him it is a slander.

33. Part of Hadith 2564a in Sahih Al-Muslim reads: A Muslim is the brother of a Muslim. He neither oppresses him nor humiliates him nor looks down upon him. The piety is here, (and while saying so) he pointed towards his chest thrice. It is a serious evil for a Muslim that he should look down upon his brother Muslim. All things of a Muslim are inviolable for his brother in faith: his blood, his wealth and his honour.

34. Al-Baqarah, Verse 256 reads: There is no compulsion in religion. The right direction is henceforth distinct from error. And he who rejecteth false deities and believeth in Allah hath grasped a firm handhold which will never break. Allah is Hearer, Knower.

35. Al-Nisa, Verse 152 reads: But those who believe in Allah and His messengers and make no distinction between any of them, unto them Allah will give their wages; and Allah was ever Forgiving, Merciful.

36. Al-Mumtahnah 60, Verse 8 reads: Allah forbiddeth you not those who warred not against you on account of religion and drove you not out from your homes, that ye should show them kindness and deal justly with them. Lo! Allah loveth the just dealers.

37. Al-Kahf 18, part of Verse 29 reads: Say: (It is) the truth from the Lord of you (all). Then whosoever will, let him believe, and whosoever will, let him disbelieve.

38. Al-Anaam, Verse 104 reads: Proofs have come unto you from your Lord, so whoso seeth, it is for his own good, and whoso is blind is blind to his own hurt. And I am not a keeper over you.

39. Al-Ghashiyah 88, Verse 21 and 22 read: Remind them, for thou art but a remembrance. Thou art not at all a warder over them.

Yunus 10, Verse 99 reads: And if thy Lord willed, all who are in the earth would have believed together. Wouldst thou (Muhammad) compel men until they are believers?

Ibid. Verse 108 reads: Say: O mankind! Now hath the Truth from your Lord come unto you. So whosoever is guided, is guided only for (the good of) his soul, and whosoever erreth, erreth only against it. And I am not a warder over you.

An-Naml 27, Verse 92 reads: And to recite the Qur'an. And whoso goeth right, goeth right only for (the good of) his own soul; and as for him who goeth astray–(Unto him) say: Lo! I am only a warner.

An-Noor, Verse 54 reads: Say: Obey Allah and obey the messenger. But if ye turn away, then (it is) for him (to do) only that wherewith he hath been charged, and for you (to do) only that wherewith ye have been charged. If ye obey him, ye will go aright. But the messenger hath no other charge than to convey (the message) plainly.

40. Al-Kafirun 109 reads: 1 Say: O disbelievers! 2 I worship not that which ye worship; 3 Nor worship ye that which I worship. 4 And I shall not worship that which ye worship. 5 Nor will ye worship that which I worship. 6 Unto you your religion, and unto me my religion.

41. The Jews of Banu 'Awf, together with Muslims, constitute an umma (group). The religion of the Jews is for themselves, the religion of Muslims for themselves. This includes both their mawla and themselves personally.

42. Ali Bulac, "The Medina Document," in *Liberal Islam: A Source Book*, ed. Charles Kurzman (New York: Oxford University Press, 1998), 172.

43. Al-Baqarah, Verse 217 reads: And whoso becometh a renegade and dieth in his disbelief: such are they whose works have fallen both in the world and the Hereafter. Such are rightful owners of the Fire: they will abide therein.

44. An-Nisa, Verse 137 reads: Lo! Those who believe, then disbelieve and then (again) believe, then disbelieve, and then increase in disbelief, Allah will never pardon them, nor will He guide them unto a way.

45. Part of Hadith 6899 in Sahih Al-Bukhari reads: Allah's Messenger (ﷺ) never killed anyone except in one of the following three situations: (1) A person who killed somebody unjustly, was killed (in Qisas,) (2) a married person who committed illegal sexual intercourse and (3) a man who fought against Allah and His Apostle and deserted Islam and became an apostate.

Part of Hadith 3017 in Sahih Al-Bukhari reads: If somebody (a Muslim) discards his religion, kill him.

46. Hadith 4328 in Ila us Sunan reads (translated from Arabic by Google): If any Muslim insults God or one of the prophets, he has lied to the Messenger of God, may God bless him and grant him peace, and it is an apostasy that should be repented. If he returns, he shall be released. Otherwise he will be killed. And whoever amongst non-Muslims protected under pact disobeys, curses God, or curses any of the prophets, and speaks out loudly; then he broke the covenant, so kill him.

47. Article 34 reads: Freedom of expression shall be inviolable. Every Afghan shall have the right to express thoughts through speech, writing, illustrations as well as other means in accordance with provisions of this constitution. Every Afghan shall have the right, according to provisions of law, to print and publish on subjects without prior submission to state authorities. Directives related to the press, radio, and television as well as publications and other mass media shall be regulated by law.

48. "Crimes against Religions," in *Penal Code* (Government of Republic of Afghanistan, 1976), 100–1.

49. "General Principles and Definitions," in *Penal Code*, 1.

50. Article 48 reads: Freedoms of expression, association and assembly shall be guaranteed to the citizen. Article 50 reads: Freedom of the press, be it written, audio-visual or on information networks shall be guaranteed. It shall not be restricted by any form of prior censorship. This freedom shall not be exploited to infringe upon the dignity, liberty and rights of the others.

51. Article 144 bis 2. (New) reads (translated from French by Google): Anyone is punished by imprisonment of three (3) years to five (5) years and one fine of fifty thousand (50,000) DA to one hundred thousand (100,000) DA, or one of these two penalties only, whoever offends the Prophet (peace and blessings be upon him) and the messengers of God or denigrates the dogma or precepts of Islam, whether in writing, drawing, statement or any other way. Criminal proceedings are initiated ex officio by the public prosecutor.

52. Article 160 (Modified) reads (translated from French by Google): Anyone is punished by imprisonment of five (5) to ten (10) years who willfully and publicly destroys, mutilates, degrades or profanes the Sacred Book.

53. *Code Penal (French)* (Republique Algerienne Democratique et Populaire).

54. Article 26 reads: National and foreign periodical and specialized publications, whatever their nature of purpose, must not contain any illustration, narrative, information or insertion contrary to Islamic morality, national values or human rights or advocate racism, fanaticism and treason. Further, such publications must contain no publicity or advertising that may promote violence and delinquency.

55. Nisrine Abiad, *Sharia, Muslim States and International Human Rights Treaty Obligations: A Comparative Study* (London: British Institute of International and Comparative Law, 2008), 83.

56. Article 77 reads: Any person who, in writing, or by sounds, images, drawings or any other direct or indirect means, offends against Islam and the other holy religions shall be punished by imprisonment of six (6) months to three (3) years and a fine of 10,000 to 50,000 DA or by one of those penalties only.

57. "People's Democratic Republic of Algeria," in *African Charter on Human and People's Rights: Fifth and Sixth Periodic Reports* (achpr.org, 2014), 15.

58. Article 23 reads: Freedom of opinion and scientific research is guaranteed. Everyone has the right to express his opinion and publish it by word of mouth, in writing or otherwise under the rules and conditions laid down by law, provided that the fundamental beliefs of Islamic doctrine are not infringed, the unity of the people is not prejudiced, and discord or sectarianism is not aroused.

59. Article 22 reads: Freedom of conscience is absolute. The State guarantees the inviolability of worship, and the freedom to perform religious rites and hold religious parades and meetings in accordance with the customs observed in the country.

60. Article 311 reads: A punishment of imprisonment for a period not exceeding one year or a fine not exceeding BD 100 shall be inflicted upon: any person who deliberately causes disturbance to the holding of religious rituals by a recognized sect or to a religious ceremony or meeting or obstructing such events or preventing the holding thereof with the use of force or threat. Any person who destroys, damages or desecrates a place of worship or a recognized sect or a symbol or other things having a religious inviolability.

61. *Bahrain Penal Code, 1976* (MENA Rights).

62. Article 309 reads: A punishment for a period not exceeding one year or a fine not exceeding BD 100 shall be inflicted upon any person who commits an offence by any method of expression against one of the recognized religious sects or ridicules the rituals thereof.

63. Article 310 reads: The punishment provided for in the preceding Article shall be inflicted: upon any person who prints or publishes a holy book for members of a recognized religious sect should he deliberately alters the text thereof in a manner aiming at changing the meanings thereof or ridiculing its teachings and principles. Upon any person who commits in public an insult against a symbol or a person being glorified or considered sacred to members of a particular sect. upon any person who imitates in public a religious ritual or ceremony with the intention of ridiculing it.

64. *Bahrain Penal Code.*

65. Article 39 reads: (1) Freedom of thought and conscience is guaranteed. (2) Subject to any reasonable restrictions imposed by law in the interests of the security of the State, friendly relations with foreign states, public order, decency or morality, or in relation to contempt of court, defamation or incitement to an offence—(a) the right of every citizen to freedom of speech and expression; and (b) freedom of the press, are guaranteed.

66. Article 41 reads: (1) Subject to law, public order and morality – (a) every citizen has the right to profess, ractice or propagate any religion; (b) every religious community or denomination has the right to establish, maintain and manage its religious institutions. (2) No person attending any educational institution shall be required to receive religious instruction, or to take part in or to attend any religious ceremony or worship, if that instruction, ceremony or worship relates to a religion other than his own.

67. Article 295A reads: Whoever, with deliberate and malicious intention of outraging the religious feelings of any class of the citizens of Bangladesh, by words, either spoken or written, or by visible representations insults or attempts to insult the religion or the religious beliefs of that class, shall be punished with imprisonment of either description for a term which may extend to two years, or with fine, or with both.

68. Article 298 reads: Whoever, with the deliberate intention of wounding the religious feelings of any person, utters any word or makes any sound in the hearing of that person or makes any gesture in the sight of that person or places any object in the sight of that person, shall be punished with imprisonment of either description for a term which may extend to one year, or with fine, or with both.

69. *The Penal Code* (Laws of Bangladesh, 1860).

70. Part of Article 1 reads: All other religions may be racticed in peace and harmony by the persons professing them.

71. Article 108 reads: (1) Any Muslim who declares himself or any other person as god … shall be liable on conviction to death as hadd. (2) Any Muslim who declares himself or any other person as god and it is proved by evidence other than those provided under subsection (1) … shall be liable on conviction to imprisonment for a term not exceeding 30 years and whipping not exceeding 40 strokes.

72. Article 109 reads: (1) Any Muslim who declares himself or any other person as Rasul or Nabi. . . shall be liable on conviction to death as hadd. (2) Any Muslim who declares himself or any other person as Rasul or Nabi and it is proved by evidence other than those provided under subsection (1) . . . shall be liable on conviction to imprisonment for a term not exceeding 30 years and whipping not exceeding 40 strokes.

73. Article 110 reads: Any Muslim who contempts or brings into contempt Nabi Muhammad Sallallahu 'Alaihi Wa Sallam or any Nabi Allah . . .shall be liable on conviction to death as hadd. (2) Any Muslim who contempts or brings into contempt Nabi Muhammad Sallallahu 'Alaihi Wa Sallam or any Nabi Allah and it is proved by evidence other than those provided under subsection (1) . . . shall be liable on conviction to imprisonment for a term not exceeding 30 years and whipping not exceeding 40 strokes.

74. Article 111 reads: (1) Any Muslim who- (a) derides, mocks, mimics, ridicules or insults any verse of the Al-Qur'an or hadith of Nabi Muhammad Sallallahu 'Alaihi Wa Sallam; (b) denies the hadith of Nabi Muhammad Sallallahu 'Alaihi Wa Sallam as a source or authority (hujjiyyah) of the teachings of the religion of Islam; or (c) denies obligatory matters with ijma', . . . shall be liable on conviction to death as hadd. (2) . . . is proved by evidence other than those provided under subsection (1) is guilty of the offence of irtidad and shall be liable on conviction to imprisonment for a term not exceeding 30 years and whipping not exceeding 40 strokes.

75 Article 112 reads: (1) Any Muslim who declares himself as a non-Muslim . . . shall be liable on conviction to death as hadd. (2) Any Muslim who declares himself as a non-Muslim and it is proved by evidence other than those provided under subsection (1) . . . shall be liable on conviction to imprisonment for a term not exceeding 30 years and whipping not exceeding 40 strokes.

76. *Syariah Penal Code Order, 2013* (Brunei Darussalam Government Gazette, 2013), 1718–19.

77. Article 45 reads: Freedom of thought and opinion shall be guaranteed. Every individual has the right to express an opinion and to disseminate it verbally, in writing or illustration, or by any other means of publication and expression.

78. Article 43 reads: Freedom of belief is an inviolable right. The State shall guarantee the freedom to practice religious rites and to establish places of worship for the divine religions, as regulated by law.

79. Article 44 reads: Insult or abuse of all religious messengers and prophets shall be prohibited.

80. *The Constitution of the Arab Republic of Egypt.*

81. Article 98F reads: Detention for a period of not less than six months and not exceeding five years, or paying a fine of not less than five hundred pounds and not exceeding one thousand pounds shall be the penalty inflicted on whoever exploits and uses the religion in advocating and propagating by talk or in writing, or by any other method, extremist thoughts with the aim of instigating sedition and division or disdaining and contempting any of the heavenly religions or the sects belonging thereto, or prejudicing national unity or social peace.

82. *Criminal Code of Egypt* (UNODC), 1937.

83. Article 28 reads: The freedom to associate and to assemble, to express written and oral opinions, etc., shall be regulated by law. Article 28E(3) reads: Every person shall have the right to the freedom to associate, to assemble and to express opinions.

84. Article 28E(1) reads: Every person shall be free to choose and to practice the religion of his/her choice. Article 28E(2) reads: Every person shall have the right to the freedom to believe his/her faith (kepercayaan). Article 29(2) reads: The State guarantees all persons the freedom of worship, each according to his/her own religion or belief.

85. Article 156(a) reads: By a maximum imprisonment of five years shall be punished any person who deliberately in public gives expression to feelings or commits an act, a) which principally have the character of being at enmity with, abusing or staining a religion, adhered to in Indonesia; b) with the intention to prevent a person to adhere to any religion based on the belief of the almighty God.

86. *Penal Code of Indonesia* (Jakarta: Ministry of Justice, 1982), 42.

87. Article 24 reads: Publications and the press have freedom of expression, except when it is detrimental to the fundamental principles of Islam or the rights of the public, and the details will be specified by law. Article 175 reads: The freedom of expression and dissemination of ideas must be secure in the Radio and Television of the Islamic Republic of Iran with due observance of Islamic norms and the country's interests.

88. Article 14 reads: In compliance with the noble verse [of the Qur'an]: (God does not forbid you from dealing kindly and justly with those who have not fought with you because of your religion and who did not expel you from your homes, [60:80]) the government of the Islamic Republic of Iran and Muslims have the duty to treat non-Muslims in accordance with ethical norms and Islamic justice and fairness and to observe their human rights. This article applies to those who do not engage in conspiracy and hostile measures against Islam and the Islamic Republic of Iran.

89. Article 513 reads: Anyone who insults the sacred values of Islam or any of the Great Prophets or [twelve] Shi'ite Imams or the Holy Fatima, if considered as Saab ul-nabi [as having committed actions warranting the ad punishment for insulting the Prophet], shall be executed; otherwise, they shall be sentenced to one to five years' imprisonment.

90. Article 514 reads: Anyone who, by any means, insults Imam Khomeini, the founder of the Islamic Republic, and/or the Supreme Leader shall be sentenced to six months to two years' imprisonment.

91. *Islamic Penal Code of the Islamic Republic of Iran – Book Five* (Islamic Republic of Iran, 1996).

92. Article 6 reads: The print media are permitted to publish news items except in cases when they violate Islamic principles and codes and public rights as outlined in this chapter. Article 26 reads: Whoever insults Islam and its sanctities through the press and his/her guilt amounts to apostasy, shall be sentenced as an apostate and should his/her offense fall short of apostasy he/she shall be subject to the Islamic penal code.

93. "Press Law (Iran)," March 19, 1986.

94. Article 38 reads: The State shall guarantee in a way that does not violate public order and morality: First. Freedom of expression using all means. Second. Freedom of press, printing, advertisement, media and publication.

95. Second part of Article 2 reads: This Constitution guarantees the Islamic identity of the majority of the Iraqi people and guarantees the full religious rights to freedom of religious belief and practice of all individuals such as Christians, Yazidis, and Mandean Sabeans. Article 41 reads: Iraqis are free in their commitment to their personal status according to their religions, sects, beliefs, or choices, and this shall be regulated by law. Article 42 reads: Each individual shall have the freedom of thought, conscience, and belief.

96. Paragraph 372 reads: The following persons are punishable by a period of detention not exceeding 3 years or by a fine not exceeding 100 dinars: (1) Any person who attacks the creed of a religious minority or pours scorn on its religious practices. (4) Any person who prints or publishes a book sacred to a religious minority and deliberately misspells the texts so that the meaning of the text is altered or who makes light of its tenets or teachings. (5) Any person who publicly insults a symbol or a person who constitutes an object of sanctification, worship or reverence to a religious minority. (6) Any person who publicly imitates a religious ceremony or celebration with intent to deceive.

97. *The Penal Code (Iraq)* (Ministry of Justice, 1969), 125.

98. Article 15(i) reads: The State shall guarantee freedom of opinion. Every Jordanian shall be free to express his opinion by speech, in writing, or by means of photographic representation and other forms of expression, provided that such does not violate the law.

99. Article 14 reads: The State shall safeguard the free exercise of all forms of worship and religious rites in accordance with the customs observed in the Kingdom, unless such is inconsistent with public order or morality.

100. Article 273 reads: Whoever dares to publicly scorn or curse any of the profits, he / she shall be punished by imprisonment from one to three years.

101. Article 278 reads: Whoever commits one of the following acts, he / she shall be punished by imprisonment for a period not to exceed three months or a fine not to exceed twenty dinars (JD20): 1. Publishes any print, writing, picture or effigy calculated or tending to outrage the religious feelings or belief of other persons, or; 2. Utters in a public place and in the hearing of another person any word or sound calculated or tending to outrage the religious feelings or belief of such person.

102. "The Penal Code for the Year 1960 (Jordan)," MENARights.org.

103. Article 5 reads: Publications shall respect the truth and refrain from publishing anything that conflicts with the principles of freedom, national responsibility, human rights, and values of the Arab and Islamic nation.

104. "Jordan: Press and Publications Law," Al-Bab.com.

105. Article 36 reads (translated online): Freedom of opinion and scientific research is guaranteed, and every person has the right to express and publish his opinion by speech, writing, or otherwise, in accordance with the terms and conditions stipulated by the law.

106. Article 35 reads (translated online): Freedom of belief is absolute, and the state protects the freedom to perform religious rites in accordance with established customs, provided that it does not violate public order or contradict morals.

107. Article 111 reads: Anyone who, in one of the public ways set out in article 101, broadcasts opinions that include ridicule, contempt or reduction of religion or religious denomination, whether by contesting his or her beliefs, rituals, rituals or teachings, shall be liable to imprisonment for a term not exceeding one year and to a fine not exceeding 1,000 dinars or one of those penalties.

108. "Kuwaiti Penal Code no. 16/1960," aalawyer.co.

109. Article 19 reads: It shall be prohibited to meddle in matters related to God, the Holy Quran, Prophets, the Noble Companions of Prophet Muhammad, Wives of the Prophet, peace be upon him, or persons who are part of the Prophet's family, peace be upon them, by meddling, defamation, slander, or mocking in any forms of expression that are stipulated under Article (29) of the Law No (31) for the year 1970 on Amendment of Some of the Provisions of the Penalty Law No (16) for the year 1960.

110. "Law No (3) for the Year 2006 on Press and Publications (Kuwait)," MENARights.com.

111. Article 14 reads: The State shall guarantee freedom of opinion, individual and collective expression, research, communication, press, media, printing and editing, movement, assembly, demonstration and peaceful sit-in in accordance with the statute.

112. Part of Article 1 reads: The State shall guarantee for non-Muslims the freedom to practice their religious rituals.

113. Article 291 reads: Anyone who publicly attacks the Islamic religion, which is the official religion of the State according to the Constitution of Libya, through expressions that are inappropriate for God, prophets, or messengers, shall be punished by a penalty of detention for a period not exceeding two years.

114. Article 289 reads: Anyone who interferes with the performance of a religious rite that is publicly performed or with the relevant religious celebration, or who hinders the same by violence or threats, shall be punished by detention for a period not exceeding one year or a fine not exceeding LYD 50. The same penalty shall apply to anyone who destroys, breaks, damages, or desecrates buildings designated for the performance of religious rites, or other items that are sacred to members of a religious sect or to any section of the country's inhabitants.

115. Article 290 reads: The penalty prescribed by the previous article shall apply to anyone who attacks, by any means of publicity, any religious faith that publicly performs its rites. The following shall fall under the provisions of this article: 1. Printing or publishing a book considered sacred by any religious sect that performs its rites publicly, if the text of the book is intentionally distorted so as to give the same a different meaning. 2. Imitation of a religious ceremony or religious rite in a public assembly for the purpose of ridicule or amusing the public.

116. *Penal Code* (Libyan Security Sector Legislation), 65.

117. Article 10(1)a reads: Every citizen has the right to freedom of speech and expression.

118. Article 11(1) reads: Every person has the right to profess and ractice his religion and, subject to Clause (4), to propagate it. Clause (4) of Article 11 reads: State law and in respect of the Federal Territories of Kuala Lumpur, Labuan and Putrajaya, federal law may control or restrict the propagation of any religious doctrine or belief among persons professing the religion of Islam.

119. Section 295 reads: Whoever destroys, damages or defiles any place of worship, or any object held sacred by any class of persons, with the intention of thereby insulting the religion of any class of persons, or with the knowledge that any class of persons is likely to consider such destruction, damage or defilement as an insult to their religion, shall be punished with imprisonment for a term which may extend to two years or with fine or with both.

120. Section 298 reads: Whoever, with deliberate intention of wounding the religious feelings of any person, utters any word or makes any sound in the hearing of that person, or makes any gesture in the sight of that person, or places any object in the sight of that person, shall be punished with imprisonment for a term which may extend to one year or with fine or with both. Section 298A. (1) reads: Whoever by words, either spoken or written, or by signs, or by visible representations, or by any act, activity or conduct, or by organizing, promoting or arranging, or assisting in organizing, promoting or arranging, any activity, or otherwise in any other manner—(a) causes, or attempts to cause, or is likely to cause disharmony, disunity, or feelings of enmity, hatred or ill will; or (b) prejudices, or attempts to prejudice, or is likely to prejudice, the maintenance of harmony or unity, on grounds of religion, between persons or groups of persons professing the same or different religions, shall be punished with imprisonment for a term of not less than two years and not more than five years.

121. *Act 547 Penal Code* (Government of Malaysia, 1997), 167–68.

122. Article 27 reads: Everyone has the right to freedom of thought and the freedom to communicate opinions and expression in a manner that is not contrary to any tenet of Islam.

123. Part of Section 617 reads: A person commits an offense if (1) engages in religious oration and criticism of Islam in public or in a public medium with the intention to cause disregard for Islam; or (2) produces, sells, distributes, or offers material criticizing Islam with the intention to cause disregard to Islam.

124. *Maldives Law No 6/2014 Penal Code* (University of Pennsylvania, 2014).

125. Part of Article 10 reads: The State guarantees to all citizens the public and individual freedoms, notably: the freedom of opinion and of thought; the freedom of expression.

126. Part of Article 306 reads (translated from French by Google): Anyone who has committed a public outrage against decency and morals of Islam or has violated sacred places or helped to violate them, . . . will be punished with a correctional sentence of three months to two years imprisonment and a fine of 5,000 to 60,000 UM. Any Muslim guilty of the crime of apostasy, . . . he is condemned to death as an apostate, and his property will be confiscated.

127. *Ordonnance 83-162 Du 09 Juillet 1983 Portant Institution D'un Code Pénal* (Journal Officiel de la République Islamique de Mauritanie, 1984), 62.

128. Part of Article 25 reads: The freedoms of thought, of opinion and of expression under all their form(s) are guaranteed. Part of Article 28 reads: The freedom of the press is guaranteed and may not be limited by any form of prior censure. All have the right to express and to disseminate freely and within the sole limits expressly provided by the law, information, ideas and opinions.

129. Article 3 reads: Islam is the religion of the State, which guarantees to all the free exercise of beliefs (cultes).

130. Article 220 reads: Anyone who, by violence or threats, has coerced or prevented one or more people from exercising a cult, or from attending the exercise of this cult, is punished by imprisonment of six months to three years and a fine of 200 to 500 dirhams. Same penalty is given to whoever uses means of seduction in order to shake the faith of a Muslim or to convert him to another religion, either by exploiting its weakness or its needs, or by using for these purposes educational establishments, health, asylums or orphanages. In the event of a conviction, the closure of the establishment which was used to commit the offense may be ordered, either definitively, or for a period which may not exceed three years.

131. *Code Penal (Morocco)* (Ministry of Justice and Liberty, 2011), 78.

132. Article 29 reads: The freedom of opinion and the expression thereof through speech, writing and other means of expression is guaranteed within the limits of the Law.

133. Article 28 reads: The freedom to practice religious rites according to recognised customs is protected, provided it does not violate the public order or contradict morals.

134. Article 269 reads: Whoever commits any of the following acts shall be punished by imprisonment for a period no less than (3) three years and not exceeding (10) ten years: (a) disrespecting or offending the divine verbally, in writing, by drawing, by gesturing, or by using any other means. (b) offending, distorting, or desecrating the Holy Quran. (c) offending the religion of Islam or any of its rites, or insulting an Abrahamic religion. (d) disrespecting or offending any of the prophets verbally, in writing, by drawing, by gesturing, or by using any other means. (e) sabotaging or desecrating buildings, or any of their contents, if prepared to conduct religious rites of Islam or those of other Abrahamic religions.

135. Article 273 reads: Whoever produces, creates, sells, displays for sale or circulation, obtains, or possesses products, goods, publications, tapes, or any other material carrying drawings, logos, words, symbols, signs, or anything else offensive to the religion of Islam or another Abrahamic religion, or advertises them with knowledge thereof, shall be punished by imprisonment for a period no less than (10) ten days and not exceeding a year, and a fine no less than (100) one hundred Rial Omani and not exceeding (1,000) one thousand Rial Omani, or one of those two punishments.

136. *The (Omani) Penal Law Promulgated by Royal Decree 7/2018* (Ministry of Justice and Legal Affairs, 2018), 66–67.

137. Article 19 reads: Every citizen shall have the right to freedom of speech and expression, and there shall be freedom of the press, subject to any reasonable restrictions imposed by law in the interest of the glory of Islam or the integrity, security or defence of Pakistan or any part thereof, friendly relations with foreign States, public

order, decency or morality, or in relation to contempt of court, (commission of) or incitement to an offence.

138. Article 20 reads: Subject to law, public order and morality,— (a) every citizen shall have the right to profess, practice and propagate his religion; and (b) every religious denomination and every sect thereof shall have the right to establish, maintain and manage its religious institutions.

139. Article 295 reads: Whoever destroys, damages or defiles any place of worship, or any object held sacred by any class of persons with the intention of thereby insulting the religion of any class of persons or with the knowledge that any class of persons is likely to consider such destruction damage or defilement as an insult to their religion. Shall be punished with imprisonment of either description for a term which may extend to two years, or with fine,

or with both.

140. Article 295A reads: Whoever, with deliberate and malicious intention of outraging the 'religious feelings of any class of the citizens of Pakistan, by words, either spoken or written, or by visible representations insults the religion or the religious beliefs of that class, shall be punished with imprisonment of either description for a term which may extend to ten years, or with fine, or with both.

141. Article 295B reads: Whoever willfully defiles, damages or desecrates a copy of the Holy Qur'an or of an extract therefrom or uses it in any derogatory manner or for any unlawful purpose shall be punishable with imprisonment for life.

142. Article 295C reads: Whoever by words, either spoken or written, or by visible representation or by any imputation, innuendo, or insinuation, directly or indirectly, defiles the sacred name of the Holy Prophet Muhammad (peace be upon him) shall be punished with death, or imprisonment for life, and shall also be liable to fine.

143. Article 298 reads: Whoever, with the deliberate intention of wounding the religious feelings of any person, utters any word or makes any sound in the hearing of that person or makes any gesture in the sight of that person or places any object in the sight of that person, shall be punished with imprisonment of either description for a term which may extend to one year or with fine, or with both.

144. Article 298A reads: Whoever by words, either spoken or written, or by visible representation, or by any imputation, innuendo or insinuation, directly or indirectly, defiles the sacred name of any wife (Ummul Mumineen), or members of the family (Ahle-bait), of the Holy Prophet (peace be upon him), or any of the righteous Caliphs (Khulafa-e-Rashideen) or companions (Sahaaba) of the Holy Prophet (peace be upon him) shall be punished with imprisonment of either description for a term which may extend to three years, or with fine, or with both.

145. *Pakistan Penal Code (Act XLV of 1860)* (Government of Pakistan, 1860).

146. Article 47 reads: Freedom of expression of opinion and scientific research is guaranteed in accordance with the conditions and circumstances set forth in the law.

147. Article 50 reads: Freedom to practice religious rites shall be guaranteed to all persons in accordance with the law and the requirements of the maintenance of public order and morality.

148. Article 1(1) reads: Islamic Sharia provisions concerning the following crimes are applicable if the suspect or the victim is a Muslim: 1- The crimes such as theft, adultery, defamation, drinking alcohol and apostasy.

149. Article 256 reads: One is convicted to no more than seven years in prison in case of committing any of the following deeds: 1- Insulting the Supreme Being in letter and spirit, in writing, drawing, gesturing or in any other way. 2- Offending, misinterpreting or violating the Holy Koran. 3- Offending the Islamic religion or one of its rites. 4- Cursing any of the divine religions according to the regulations of the Islamic law. 5- Insulting any of the prophets in letter and spirit, in writing, drawing, gesturing or in any other way. 6- Sabotaging, breaking, damaging or violating places or their contents if they are made to perform religious rites for one of the divine religions according to the regulations of the Islamic law.

150. Article 263 reads: One is convicted to no more than a year and to a fine of no more than a thousand riyals or to one of these two penalties in case of producing, selling, exposing for sale or circulation, or possessing products, merchandise, prints or tapes including drawings, slogans, words, symbols, signals or anything else that might offend the Islamic religion or other divine religions according to the regulations of the Islamic law. The same penalty is imposed on everyone who uses disks, computer programs or magnetized tapes to offend Islam or other divine religions according to the regulations of the Islamic law.

151. *The (Qatari) Penal Code* (National Anti-Money Laundering & Terrorism Financing Committee, 2004), 6 and 59.

152. Article 39 reads: Mass media and all other vehicles of expression shall employ civil and polite language, contribute towards the education of the nation and strengthen unity. It is prohibited to commit acts leading to disorder and division, affecting the security of the state and its public relations, or undermining human dignity and rights. Details shall be specified in the Law.

153. Article 26 reads: The State shall protect human rights in accordance with the Sharia.

154. Article 18 reads: The Courts shall apply rules of the Islamic Sharia in cases that are brought before them, according to the Holy Quran and the Sunna, and according to laws which are decreed by the ruler in agreement with Holy Quran and the Sunna.

155. Part of Article 18 reads: 1. Every person has the right to have and express their opinions and to receive and impart their opinion, information and ideas in any way. 2. Freedom of expression includes freedom of speech, and freedom of the media, including all forms of electronic and web-based media.

156. Article 17 reads: 1. Every person is free to practice his or her religion. 2. No religion other than Islam can be propagated in the Federal Republic of Somalia.

157. Article 313 reads: (Bringing the Religion of the State into contempt) 1. Whoever publicly brings the religion of Islam into contempt shall be punished with imprisonment up to two years. 2. Whoever publicly insults the religion of Islam by bringing into contempt persons professing it or places or objects dedicated to worship, shall be liable to same punishment. Article 314 reads: (Disturbance of Religious Functions) Whoever impedes or disturbs the exercise of functions, ceremonies or re-

ligious practices of the Islamic faith in a place intended for the purpose, or in a public place or place open to public, shall be punished with imprisonment up to two years.

158. *Somali Penal Code* (Somali Land Law, 1962), 251–52.

159. Article 42 (2) reads: Every citizen shall have the right to freely and openly express his views whether in writing or orally or by all other means of expression.

160. Article 42 (1) reads: Freedom of belief shall be protected in accordance with the law.

161. Article 462 reads (translated by Google): Whoever in one of the methods stipulated in Article 208 denigrates religious rituals practiced overtly or exhorting contempt for one of these rites shall be punished by imprisonment from two months to two years.

162. "Syrian Penal Code (Arabic)," WIPO.int.

163. Article 31 reads: Freedom of opinion, thought, expression, information and publication shall be guaranteed. These freedoms shall not be subject to prior censorship.

164. Article 6 reads: The state is the guardian of religion. It guarantees freedom of conscience and belief, the free exercise of religious practices and the neutrality of mosques and places of worship from all partisan nstrumentalization. The state undertakes to disseminate the values of moderation and tolerance and the protection of the sacred, and the prohibition of all violations thereof. It undertakes equally to prohibit and fight against calls for Takfir and the incitement of violence and hatred.

165. Article 212bis reads (translated from French): The distribution, sale, exhibition to public view and holding for the purpose of distribution, sale, exhibition for the purpose of propaganda, leaflets, bulletins and fliers of foreign origin or name, likely to harm public order or good morals. Any infringement of the prohibition enacted by the preceding paragraph may result, in addition immediate seizure, imprisonment from 6 months to 5 years and a fine of 120 to 1,200 dinars.

166. Article 226bis reads (translated from French): Punishment of six months imprisonment and a fine of one thousand dinars shall be given to whoever publicly undermines good morals or public morals by gesture or intentionally speaking or interfering with others in a way that offends modesty. Also, to anyone who attracts public attention to an occasion of debauchery, through writings, recordings, audio or visual, electronic or optical messages.

167. *Code Penal (Tunisia) 2015* (Republic of Tunisia, 2015), 44 and 68.

168. Article 25 reads: Everyone has the freedom of thought and opinion. No one shall be compelled to reveal his/her thoughts and opinions for any reason or purpose; nor shall anyone be blamed or accused because of his/her thoughts and opinions. Article 26 reads: Everyone has the right to express and disseminate his/her thoughts and opinions by speech, in writing or in pictures or through other media, individually or collectively. This freedom includes the liberty of receiving or imparting information or ideas without interference by official authorities. This provision shall not preclude subjecting transmission by radio, television, cinema, or similar means to a system of licensing.

169. Part of Article 24 reads: Everyone has the freedom of conscience, religious belief and conviction. Acts of worship, religious rites and ceremonies shall be con-

ducted freely, as long as they do not violate the provisions of Article 14. No one shall be compelled to worship, or to participate in religious rites and ceremonies, or to reveal religious beliefs and convictions, or be blamed or accused because of his religious beliefs and convictions.

170. Part of Article 24 reads: No one shall be allowed to exploit or abuse religion or religious feelings, or things held sacred by religion, in any manner whatsoever, for the purpose of personal or political interest or influence, or for even partially basing the fundamental, social, economic, political, and legal order of the State on religious tenets.

171. Article 216(3) reads: A person who publicly degrades the religious values of a section of the public shall be sentenced to a penalty of imprisonment for a term of six months to one year, where the act is capable of disturbing public peace.

172. *Penal Code of Turkey* (Strasbourg: Council of Europe, 2016), 71.

173. Article 30 reads: Freedom of opinion and expressing it verbally, in writing or by other means of expression shall be guaranteed within the limits of law.

174. Article 32 reads: Freedom to exercise religious worship shall be guaranteed in accordance with established customs, provided that it does not conflict with public policy or violate public morals.

175. Part of Article 312 reads: Shall be sentenced to detention and/or a fin whoever perpetrates one of the following crimes: 1. Offense to any of the Islamic sacred beliefs or rites: 2. Insult to any of the divine recognized religions. Should any of these crimes be perpetrated publicly, the penalty shall be detention for a minimum period of one year in addition to a fine.

176. *UAE Penal Code* (Abu Dhabi: Judicial Department, 2011), 152.

177. Part of Article 42 reads: The state shall guarantee freedom of thought and expression of opinion in speech, writing and photography within the limits of the law.

178. Part of Article 60 reads: Defending religion and the homeland is a sacred duty.

179. Article 194 reads: To be sentenced to imprisonment for a period not exceeding three years or to a fine: First: Whoever disseminates in public ideas containing ridicule or contempt of religion in its beliefs or rituals or teachings. Second: Whoever instigates in public or ridicules a faction of people or empowers a faction to dominate for the purpose of disturbing public peace.

180. Article 195 reads: The sentence shall be imprisonment for a period not exceeding five years or a fine if the religion or the sect which is affected by ridicule or contempt or inferiority is the Islamic religion.

181. Article 259 reads: Anyone who turns back from or denounces the religion of Islam, is punished by the death penalty after being questioned for repentance three times and after giving him a respite of thirty days. The Apostasy in public by speech or acts is considered contradictory to the principles of Islam and its pillars in intention and determination. If the intention or determination is not established and the guilty shows repentance, there will be no punishment.

182. Article 260 reads: Punishment with imprisonment for a period not exceeding five years or a fine is to anyone who distorts willfully the Holy Quran in a manner which changes its meaning with the purpose of harming the natural Religion.

183. Article 261 reads: Punishment with imprisonment for a period not exceeding one year or a fine not more than two thousand Ryals will be imposed on: 1- Whoever destroys or misrepresents or profanes a mosque or any other place set up by a license from the State to perform religious rituals or a symbol or other objects having religious sanctity. 2- Whoever distorts deliberately the establishment of recognized rituals of a sect or a celebration or religious meeting or disrupts something out of that or forbids it by force or threat.

184. *Yemen: Republican Decree, by Law no. 12 for 1994, Concerning Crimes and Penalties* (Republic of Yemen, 1994).

Conclusion

SEPTEMBER 11 ATTACKS: THE TURNING POINT

The 9/11 incident resulted in an environment of mistrust and hostility between the West and the Muslim world although it was clearly evident that the majority of the Muslim population around the globe was indifferent to the perpetrators of the attacks and there was (and still is) a debate over the legitimacy of the attacks within the Islamic world as well. The majority of Islamic scholars did not endorse the act, some of them condemned it, and a small number were in favor of it. In short, it cannot be said that the Muslim world was favoring the terrorists, or it had developed a consensus to carry out such attacks, but still it was perceived adversely by the West and the same reflected in the statement of US president George W. Bush immediately after the incident declaring a "crusade." Unfortunately, the American media also fueled such emotions with mostly baseless and factually wrong information exacerbating the animosity against Muslims. This ultimately resulted in hate crimes against Muslims, and Europe also followed the same course at the time when the inquiry into the 9/11 incident was not completed and there was very little information available about the people who were behind the attacks.

But 9/11 was not the only cause of increasing anti-Muslim sentiment in the West. There was present a generally prevalent feeling among common Westerners, their leaders, and the media that Islam and Muslims cannot coexist with them and will never be able to integrate into Western societies. Also, a major part of the problem was rapid immigration of Muslims to the Western countries and consequently shrinking job opportunities and economic privileges for natives.

ATTACKS IN THE UNITED STATES—REACTION IN EUROPE

Although the 9/11 attacks took place in the United States, the situation got worse in Europe due to more than one factor:

1. Europe is not a single country like the United States with one nation and coherent laws and social norms.
2. Despite the age of Renaissance and enlightenment, different nations within Europe were still polarized and biased.
3. Every country has different geographic, demographic, political, and social factors.
4. Economic conditions of every nation were different and fears regarding job security and economic meltdown due to immigrants were not the same.
5. Lack of cohesive laws and social structure at the continental level increased polarization and response of every nation to the emerging "threat" of Muslim immigrants.

WHY FREEDOM OF EXPRESSION IS AT THE CORE OF CONTROVERSY

This was the time when Islam and the Muslim world were openly declared a threat to Judeo-Christian heritage mostly by the media and some political leaders too. The term "Islamophobia" became prominent, and Islam and Muslims were perceived to be opposers of the notion of freedom adopted by the West over the centuries. This feeling transcended into the masses and there developed a need to protect and preserve Western norms, cultures, and values against the threat of "Islamism" (i.e., political Islam). Hate crimes and discrimination at every level against Muslims increased in Europe as well and it was thought to be a duty by many to save their right to liberty and freedom through various means against the potential danger. Ultimately, there were different forms of "expression" adopted to strengthen the Western notion of freedom of expression and to fight Muslim invasion mainly due to two reasons:

1. Freedom of expression was the right seen as most vulnerable by many in Europe because of Muslim resistance and their observance of limitations to that right according to Islamic law.
2. It was comparatively easier to act against Islam and Muslims using the right to freedom of expression than resorting to violent means and/or physical attacks, etc.

Therefore, a number of incidents began to take place and certain publications and broadcasts were made to defy Muslims. The first major attempt among those was the Dutch film controversy.

MERELY A DUTCH "FILM" AND "CARTOON" CONTROVERSY OR MORE?

As we have taken a detailed account of what the Netherlands went through before making of the controversial films affecting Muslims, it clearly proves the hypothesis with the following valid points:

1. Part of Dutch society was already antagonized against immigrants.
2. The 9/11 attacks and their aftermath turned that part specifically hostile toward Muslim immigrants.
3. Smaller sections of the media and few politicians took advantage of the situation and rose to prominence creating a hostile environment against Islam and Muslims.
4. Freedom of expression was thought to be the easiest tool to be used against Islam as Muslims are too sensitive about their religion and the Prophet.
5. Muslims in general reacted with no violent means but one person killed a politician thus resurrecting the controversy.

DANISH CARTOON CONTROVERSY: GLOBALIZING THE DEBATE

The *Jyllands-Posten* caricatures seem to be a single isolated event when compared to the Dutch episode, but it also had sociopolitical and economic connotations. It is evident by the facts we gathered in the relevant chapter that:

1. Danish society was already critical of immigrants especially Muslims.
2. The events of 9/11 strengthened this perception.
3. Anti-immigrant and anti-Muslim forces were present on the Danish political arena before 9/11.
4. Sections of the media, especially *Jyllands-Posten*, was already attacking immigrants, specifically Muslims.
5. Freedom of expression against Muslims was again perceived to be both easier and effective to antagonize Muslims and highlight them as aliens to the society.

6. Muslims were already facing economic disparity and deprivation in Denmark.
7. Interestingly in this case, Muslims in Denmark did not embark on violent means, invoked legal remedies and tried political engagements.
8. Danish political leadership, society, and the media failed to understand emotions of their fellow Muslim countrymen and to give due importance to their stance.
9. This resulted in a worldwide backlash within the Muslim world.
10. Adamance on both sides consequently made it an international crisis and point of debate.

THE *CHARLIE HEBDO* EPISODE: THE THIRD DIMENSION

The French satirical magazine was not behind, but rather ahead, of *Jyllands-Posten* in keeping Muslims at its target way before 9/11. But its case is different and termed third dimension because:

1. In the Netherlands a politician was killed but no media outlet was attacked.
2. In Denmark legal and political means were adopted against *Jyllands-Posten* but did not yield desired results for Muslims thus a global controversy was generated.
3. In France no one was killed initially, but legal and political course was adopted by Muslims and ultimately *Charlie Hebdo* offices were attacked resulting in a much bigger crisis at international level.

But again a few important points are worthy to note:

1. France experienced the largest Muslim population in Western Europe for decades.
2. French society was harmonized in general, but the scarf controversy was one of the first to be noted in the continent relating to Muslims.
3. Muslims gradually started feeling cornered during the 1990s and by the time 9/11 happened, even the government had to realize this problem.
4. Stigmatization of Islam and Muslims gradually stepped up in French society, media, and to some extent in political landscape too.
5. Muslims did not respond violently for quite some time but failed to respond academically and socially as well.
6. French courts and the government vindicated *Charlie Hebdo* failing to consider Muslim viewpoints.
7. *Charlie Hebdo* offices were stormed fueling an already much-heated debate about freedom of expression and Muslims.

FREEDOM OF EXPRESSION IN EUROPE: LIMITED OR ABSOLUTE?

One of the main points of inquiry during the research was: Is freedom of expression an absolute right given to the people across Europe? The answer to this question is tricky: In perception, we can say yes—meaning it is seemed or perceived to be absolute. Generally, it is believed that everyone, in at least the Western Hemisphere, has the liberty to express whatever they want. In theory, we will have to say no because we have hate speech laws, blasphemy regulations, and Holocaust denial punishments in the majority of countries. There might be some strong arguments supporting the laws penalizing Holocaust denial, etc., but by having these laws effective in letter and spirit, freedom of expression cannot be regarded absolute in respective countries. The point is if you can question anything then let it be anything. If you bar someone from questioning a particular thing, you will have to bar someone else from questioning something else, too, that might affect somebody.

In practical terms, we will have to take a break and ponder. This is the area that is absolutely grey almost throughout the continent and especially in the countries where controversies arose. The research in the preceding chapters tries to answer this part of the question and both perspectives are given adequate space.

HARM PRINCIPLE, OFFENSE PRINCIPLE, MUSLIMS, AND EUROPE

We have discussed limitations to freedom of expression and its legal and theoretical dimensions within the West and Europe in particular. Now another important question in this regard is: Have the principles limiting free speech and laws regulating hate speech been applied correctly to the controversies relating to Muslims in Europe? Unfortunately, in most cases Europe has remained unable to adapt to the ideological and legal standards the West has set.

RELIGIOUS BLASPHEMY VERSUS SOVEREIGN IMMUNITY

As surveyed in detail, several European nations have blasphemy laws, and many states give sovereign immunity to the monarch, etc. This concept of sovereign immunity also generates a debate: Is it fair to have and defend sovereign immunity laws but not religious blasphemy laws? This question has multiple possible answers in defense of sovereign immunity:

- Sovereign immunity is different from religious blasphemy in its nature and scope altogether.
- Legal injunctions protecting sovereign immunity are seldom invoked unlike religious blasphemy laws.
- Severity of the punishment is also a major mark of difference between the two laws.

On the other hand, those who vindicate religious blasphemy law can answer a bit differently:

- Every society has its own norms and regulations. European societies are majorly secular with no preference to religion. If sovereign immunity laws are justifiable in those societies, then religious blasphemy laws can also be justified for the people who profess a religion and do not want to get hurt or insulted.
- Sovereigns are also seldom insulted or taken to the courts, but religion often comes on target and thus blasphemy laws are invoked.
- Importance of religion for its followers is far more than sovereign for its people, thus punishments are severe in nature.

HOLOCAUST DENIAL VERSUS RELIGIOUS BLASPHEMY

Several European states have strict laws against Holocaust denial and the European Union has also legislated in this direction. Muslims raised question why the EU did not make laws regulating hate crimes against Muslims. Baltic states, too, as mentioned in the relevant chapter, wanted to have laws against denial of atrocities committed by Stalin, but it could not materialize them. There is a pertinent question that if European countries and European Union itself can have laws banning denial of the Holocaust then why cannot they have legislation prohibiting hate speech against Muslims and followers of other religions?

- If it is said that the Holocaust was a reality and reality cannot be denied, then the same goes for the religions having billions of followers.
- If questioning a religion is permissible, then how can questioning a historical event named the Holocaust not permissible?
- If questioning or denying the Holocaust hurts the feelings of the survivors, then definitely questioning or denying any religion would hurt the feelings of the followers as well.

MUSLIMS IN EUROPE: PART OF THE PROBLEM OR PART OF THE SOLUTION?

Muslims are generally deemed as part of the problem, not part of the solution within the continent of Europe. No serious efforts have been made to engage the Muslim population in combating extremism and violation of societal norms by states, courts, and societies. It is evident that on the eve of almost every controversy, Muslims resorted to find legal remedies and sociopolitical solutions. But this mindset of seeing Muslims as part of the problem obstructs the amicable resolution of disputes. The term "Islamophobia" is widely used all across the media and sociopolitical landscape and we find no phobia of any other religion at this level whatsoever. Several countries have Muslim-specific laws that ultimately generate the question: Why are only adherents of Islam targeted? Other religious factions, especially Jews and Sikhs, are seldom hurt but the proportion is not significant. This sense of alienation and targeting leaves Muslims more vulnerable and desperate to save and serve their religion.

WHY A SURVEY OF LAWS IN THE MUSLIM WORLD?

A detailed survey of laws relating to freedom of expression, freedom of religion, and blasphemy/apostasy in the Muslim world is done in order to paint a complete picture of the other side of debate. Primarily, it has few important objectives:

- To have a comprehensive view on the Islamic laws on freedom of expression, freedom of religion, and blasphemy/apostasy
- To mention the primary sources of Islamic legislation, that is, the Qur'an and Hadith, on above issues
- To explore reasoning behind the laws regulating blasphemy and apostasy in the Muslim world

Having a detailed legal narrative of both the European nations and Muslim countries, we can understand the basic differences on the ideological foundations of freedom of expression, freedom of religion, and blasphemy/apostasy.

DOES ONLY THE MUSLIM WORLD HAVE BLASPHEMY LAWS?

According to the US Commission on International Religious Freedom, not only Muslim countries but seventy-one countries worldwide have blasphemy laws including important European countries (see figure C.1).

Figure C.1. Seventy-one countries that have blasphemy laws.

Source: https://www.uscirf.gov/publication/violating-rights-enforcing-worlds-blasphemy-laws

RESEARCH FINDINGS

1. There was a general feeling of hatred and mistrust against immigrants, especially Muslims in the West as a whole and Europe in particular before 9/11.
2. The 9/11 attacks exacerbated the situation and Muslims became the prime target of hate crimes in the West and Europe in particular.
3. Europe saw more hatred and discrimination because of different laws, different sociopolitical norms, and different economic conditions, etc. nation-wise.
4. It is evident that Muslims are still the prime target leaving other religious and ethnic groups behind.
5. There is a serious lack of understanding about Islamic laws and culture among European masses, media, politicians, and even academia.

6. Media unfortunately fueled the debate rather than giving Muslims space to clarify themselves.
7. Media outlets that became the hub of controversy were already biased against Muslims for years before the respective incidents.
8. Politicians who campaigned against Islam and its adherents were already having roots within their respective cultures, 9/11 gave them a ground to surface with controversies.
9. Violent Muslim reaction proved to be counterproductive for their cause and did not have the support of the majority of Muslims, rather it was condemned.
10. Muslim efforts to resort to political and legal remedies for the resolution of controversies were usually in vain.
11. Subsequent failure of the European nations to respond with positivity and understanding to the concerns of Muslims increased the level of mistrust and pessimism among Muslims.
12. It is proven that freedom of expression and its usage was at the core of almost every controversy related to Muslims in Europe.
13. Muslim reaction and protest were met with more reaction and restrictions by European societies and governments that deteriorated the situation and planted more mistrust.
14. "Harm principle," "offense principle," and principles like "remedy to bad speech is more speech" were not adopted. Instead, it was tried to put more legal and sociopolitical restrictions on Muslims in Europe rather than having a dialogue and effort to understand.
15. No serious effort is seen by both European nations and Muslims to understand each other's viewpoints and engage in dialogue that became the real bone of contention.
16. Laws limiting freedom of expression in the name of sovereign immunity and against Holocaust denial, etc. leave questions on the freedom and limitation of expression in Europe. This generates a sense of inequality, discrimination, and alienation among religious minorities especially Muslims.
17. Muslims in the West and Europe in particular are taken for granted as part of the problem. No serious efforts are being made to try to count them as part of the solution.
18. Freedom of religion is also a burning question in today's Europe with several judgments by the courts and legislation by different nations.
19. Religion has a very little space in today's Europe while Muslims give it core importance in their everyday life and hence the clash begins.
20. Islamic law on blasphemy and apostasy is also widely debated within the Muslim world.

21. Several Muslim countries have based their blasphemy and apostasy laws on the injunctions of the Qur'an and Sunnah on which there is wider consensus.
22. There is no Islamic injunction or state law that permits an individual to punish anyone committing blasphemy and/or apostasy.
23. Around seventy countries have blasphemy laws on the books with fluctuating severity though majority of those are Muslim.
24. Continuous lack of debate between Europe (and West as a whole) and the Muslim world on freedom of expression can lead to more disastrous events.

Effort is required from both sides for better coexistence, understanding, and integration and the only way forward is dialogue.

Bibliography

Abiad, Nisrine. *Sharia, Muslim States and International Human Rights Treaty Obligations: A Comparative Study*. London: British Institute of International and Comparative Law, 2008.

Aksan, Virginia. *Ottoman Wars, 1700–1860: An Empire Besieged*. London: Pearson Education Ltd., 2007.

Al-Bab. "Jordan: Press and Publications Law." Accessed March 8, 2021. https://al-bab.com/documents-section/jordan-press-and-publications-law#:~:text=Article%2011-,A.,to%20issue%20its%20press%20publications.

Allen, Chris. *Islamophobia*. New York: Routledge, 2016.

Al-Madhagi, Ahmed Noman, and Abdelrahman A. Abdrabou, trans. *The Constitution of the Republic of Yemen*. Republic of Yemen, 2001. Accessed March 14, 2021. https://www.refworld.org/pdfid/3fc4c1e94.pdf.

Altalex. "Italian Criminal Code 2020." Accessed April 13, 2020. https://www.altalex.com/documents/codici-altalex/2014/10/30/codice-penale.

Amnesty International. "Annual Report: Moldova 2013." Accessed April 9, 2020. https://www.amnestyusa.org/reports/annual-report-moldova-2013/.

________. "Bosnia and Herzegovina Must Reject Burqa Ban." September 1, 2010. Accessed April 8, 2020. https://www.amnesty.org.uk/press-releases/bosnia-and-herzegovina-must-reject-burqa-ban.

________. "France: Reaction to Court Decision to Overturn Burkini Ban." August 26, 2016. Accessed April 29, 2020. https://www.amnesty.org/en/latest/news/2016/08/france-reaction-to-court-decision-to-overturn-burkini-ban/.

________. "French Politicians Urged to Reject Ban On Full Face Veils." May 19, 2010. Accessed April 29, 2020. https://www.amnesty.org/en/press-releases/2010/05/french-politicians-urged-reject-ban-full-face-veils/.

________. "Switzerland Minaret Ban Would Breach Freedom of Religion Obligations." November 25, 2009. Accessed April 9, 2020. https://www.amnesty.org/en/latest/news/2009/11/switzerland-minaret-ban-would-breach-freedom-religion-obligations-20091125/.

Annan, Kofi. "Confronting Islamophobia: Education for Tolerance and Understanding." United Nations. December 7, 2004. Accessed April 2, 2020. http://www.un.org/press/en/2004/sgsm9637.doc.htm.

Arnold, Thomas Walker. *The Preaching of Islam: History of the Propagation of the Muslim Faith*. Westminster: Archibald Constable & Co., 1896.

Assimakopoulos, Stavros, Fabienne H. Baider, and Sharon Millar. *Online Hate Speech in the European Union: A Discourse-Analytic Perspective*. Gewerbestrasse: Springer Open, 2017.

Aurelius, Marcus. *The Meditations*. Translated by Robin Hard. Hertfordshire: Wordsworth Editions Limited, 1997.

Bąkowski, Piotr. *Holocaust Denial in Criminal Law: Legal Frameworks in Selected EU Member States.* Brussels: European Parliamentary Research Service, 2022.

Barkan, Elazar and Ariella Lang, ed. *Memory Laws and Historical Justice: The Politics of Criminalizing the Past.* Cham: Palgrave Macmillan, 2022.

Belgian House of Representatives. "The Belgian Constitution." Accessed April 12, 2020. https://www.dekamer.be/kvvcr/pdf_sections/publications/constitution/GrondwetUK.pdf.

Belavusau, Uladzislau. *Freedom of Speech: Importing European and Us Constitutional Models in Transitional Democracies*. New York: Routledge, 2013.

Bernstein, Carl. *Attacks on the Press in 2008: A Worldwide Survey by the Committee to Protect Journalists.* New York: Committee to Protect Journalists, 2009.

Bowen, John R., Christophe Bertossi, Jan Willem Duyvendak, and Mona Lena Krook, eds. *European States and their Muslim Citizens.* New York: Cambridge University Press, 2014.

Brandeis, Louis. "Whitney Vs California [1927]." Cornell Law School. Accessed April 4, 2020. https://www.law.cornell.edu/supremecourt/text/274/357.

Brocardi. "Chapter I - Criminal Code." Accessed April 13, 2020. https://www.brocardi.it/codice-penale/libro-secondo/titolo-iv/capo-i/.

Bulac, Ali. "The Medina Document." In *Liberal Islam: A Source Book*, edited by Charles Kurzman, 172. New York: Oxford University Press, 1998.

Caldwell, Christopher. "Immigration and Islam: Europe's Crisis of Faith." *Wall Street Journal*. January 16, 2015. Accessed March 27, 2021. https://www.wsj.com/articles/europe-immigration-and-islam-europes-crisis-of-faith-1421450060.

Cesari, Jocelyne, ed. *The Oxford Handbook of European Islam.* Oxford: Oxford University Press, 2014.

Chafee, Zechariah Jr. *Freedom's Prophet: Selected Writings of Zechariah Chafee*. Edited by Edward Domenic Re. New York: Oceana Publications, 1981.

Chaib, Saïla Ouald. "Local 'burqa Ban' Violates Human Rights (According to Belgian Judge)." *Strasbourg Observers* (blog). February 16, 2011. Accessed April 24, 2020. https://strasbourgobservers.com/2011/02/16/local-%E2%80%9Cburqa-ban%E2%80%9D-violates-human-rights-according-to-belgian-judge/.

Charlesworth, M. P. "Freedom of Speech in Republican Rome." *The Classical Review* 57, no. 1 (March 1943): 49.

Coke, Edward. *The Third Part of the Institutes of the Laws of England: Concerning High Treason, and Other Pleas of the Crown, and Criminall Causes*. London: M. Flesher for W. Lee, and D. Pakeman, 1644.

Cole, Jeffrey E., ed. *Ethnic Groups of Europe: An Encyclopedia*. Santa Barbara, CA: ABC-CLIO, 2011.

Committee to Protect Journalists. "Editor Jailed Over Muhammad Cartoons." January 18, 2008. Accessed April 12, 2020. https://cpj.org/2008/01/editor-jailed-over-muhammad-cartoons.php.

Constitute Project. "Constitution of Brunei Darussalam 1959 (Rev. 2006)." Accessed March 23, 2021. https://www.constituteproject.org/constitution/Brunei_2006?lang=en.

________. "Libya's Constitution of 2011." Accessed March 10, 2021. https://www.constituteproject.org/constitution/Libya_2012.pdf?lang=en.

Constitutional Court of the Hashemite Kingdom of Jordan. "Jordanian Constitution." Accessed March 8, 2021. http://www.cco.gov.jo/en-us/Jordanian-Constitutional.

Council of Europe. "Additional Protocol to the Convention On Cybercrime, Concerning the Criminalisation of Acts of a Racist and Xenophobic Nature Committed through Computer Systems." November 7, 2002. Accessed April 8, 2020. https://www.coe.int/en/web/conventions/full-list/-/conventions/rms/090000168008160f.

________. "Explanatory Report to the Additional Protocol to the Convention On Cybercrime, Concerning the Criminalisation of Acts of a Racist and Xenophobic Nature Committed through Computer Systems." January 1, 2003. Accessed April 9, 2020. https://rm.coe.int/CoERMPublicCommonSearchServices/DisplayDCTMContent?documentId=09000016800d37ae.

De Kamer (Belgian House of Representatives). "The Belgian Constitution." Accessed April 17, 2020. https://www.dekamer.be/kvvcr/pdf_sections/publications/constitution/GrondwetUK.pdf.

EU Agency for Fundamental Rights. "Basic Law for the Federal Republic of Germany." Accessed April 4, 2020. https://fra.europa.eu/en/law-reference/basic-law-federal-republic-germany-10.

EUR-Lex. "Charter of Fundamental Rights of the European Union." October 26, 2012. Accessed April 11, 2020. https://eur-lex.europa.eu/legal-content/EN/TXT/?uri=CELEX:12012P/TXT.

________. "General Framework for Equal Treatment in Employment and Occupation." November 27, 2000. Accessed April 11, 2020. https://eur-lex.europa.eu/legal-content/EN/TXT/?uri=CELEX:32000L0078.

End Blasphemy Laws. "France "blasphemy" Law Ended: 2016!" June 18, 2020. Accessed March 28, 2021. https://end-blasphemy-laws.org/countries/europe/france-abolished-its-blasphemy-law-in-2016/.

Erasmus, Desiderius. *Erasmus: The Education of a Christian Prince with the Panegyric for Archduke Philip of Austria*. Edited by Lisa Jardine. Cambridge: Cambridge University Press, 1997.

Esposito, John. *The Future of Islam*. New York: Oxford University Press, 2010.

Euractiv. “Belgium Officially Bans the Burqa.” July 14, 2011. Accessed April 6, 2020. https://www.euractiv.com/section/languages-culture/news/belgium-officially-bans-the-burqa/.

European Court of Human Rights. “E. S. vs Austria.” October 25, 2018. http://hudoc.echr.coe.int/fre?i=001-187188.

________. “European Convention On Human Rights.” November 4, 1950. Accessed April 11, 2020. https://www.echr.coe.int/Documents/Convention_ENG.pdf.

________. “Holocaust Denial Is Not Protected by the European Convention On Human Rights.” October 3, 2019. Accessed April 11, 2020. http://hudoc.echr.coe.int/eng-press?i=003-6523883-8616003.

European Union. “Framework Decision On Combating Certain Forms and Expressions of Racism and Xenophobia by Means of Criminal Law.” November 28, 2008. Accessed April 4, 2020. https://eur-lex.europa.eu/legal-content/EN/ALL/?uri=LEGISSUM:l33178.

Evangelical Lutheran Church of Finland. “Church and State.” Accessed April 18, 2020. https://evl.fi/our-work/church-and-state#f00a7bd3.

Eyerman, Ron. *The Assassination of Theo van Gogh: From Social Drama to Cultural Trauma*. Durham, NC, and London: Duke University Press, 2008.

Federal Ministry of the Interior. “Information Leaflet.” Accessed April 17, 2020. https://www.bmi.gv.at/bmi_documents/2090.pdf.

Feinberg, Joel. *Offense to Others: The Moral Limits of the Criminal Law*. Oxford: Oxford University Press, 1985.

Ferrari, Alessandro and Sabrina Pastorelli, eds. *The Burqa Affair Across Europe: Between Public and Private Space*. New York: Routledge, 2016.

Film Threat. “The Bootleg Files: Submission.” October 27, 2006. https://filmthreat.com/uncategorized/the-bootleg-files-submission.

Finkelman, Paul, ed. *Encyclopedia of American Civil Liberties*. New York: Routledge, 2006.

Finlex. “The Constitution of Finland.” Accessed April 18, 2020. https://finlex.fi/fi/laki/ajantasa/1999/19990731.

________. “The Criminal Code of Finland.” Accessed April 13, 2020. https://finlex.fi/en/laki/kaannokset/1889/en18890039.pdf.

Fish, Stanley. *There's No Such Thing as Free Speech...and It's a Good Thing Too*. New York: Oxford University Press, 1994.

Folketinget (The Danish Parliament). “My Constitutional Act.” Accessed April 17, 2020. https://www.thedanishparliament.dk/-/media/pdf/publikationer/english/my_constitutional_act_with_explanations.ashx.

French National Assembly. “Constitution of October 4, 1958.” Accessed April 18, 2020. http://www2.assemblee-nationale.fr/langues/welcome-to-the-english-web-site-of-the-french-national-assembly#node_9440.

Gaeta, Paola, ed. *The Un Genocide Convention: A Commentary*. New York: Oxford University Press, 2009.

Government of France. “French Islam: Adapting the Law of 1905 to the World of 2018.” December 10, 2018. Accessed April 18, 2020. https://www.gouvernement.fr/en/french-islam-adapting-the-law-of-1905-to-the-world-of-2018.

Government of the Netherlands. "The Constitution of the Kingdom of the Netherlands 2018." Accessed April 10, 2020. https://www.government.nl/documents/reports/2019/02/28/the-constitution-of-the-kingdom-of-the-netherlands.

Haas, Michael. *International Human Rights: A Comprehensive Introduction*. New York: Routledge, 2014.

Hare, Ivan, and James Weinstein, eds. *Extreme Speech and Democracy*. New York: Oxford University Press, 2010.

Hariharan, Githa. *Almost Home: Finding a Place in the World from Kashmir to New York*. New York: Restless Books, 2014.

Haynes, Jeffrey ed. *Routledge Handbook of Religion and Politics*. Oxford: Routledge, 2009.

Hayworth, Alan. *Free Speech*. New York: Routledge, 2002.

Heller, Brittan, and Joris van Hoboken. *Freedom of Expression: A Comparative Summary of United States and European Law*. Amsterdam: Transatlantic Working Group, 2019.

Hennebel, Ludovic, and Thomas Hochmann, eds. *Genocide Denials and the Law*. New York: Oxford University Press, 2011.

Hervik, Peter. *The Annoying Difference: The Emergence of Danish Neonationalism, Neoracism, and Populism in the Post-1989 World*. New York: Berghahn Books, 2011.

________. *Current Themes in Imer Research: The Danish Muhammad Cartoon Conflict*. Malmo: Malmo University, 2012.

Hirsi Ali, Ayaan. *Infidel*. New York: Free Press, 2007.

Holmes, Oliver Wendell. "Abrams v. United States." Cornell Law School. November 10, 1919. Accessed April 4, 2020. https://www.law.cornell.edu/supremecourt/text/250/616.

Holocaust Remembrance Project. "Slovakia." Accessed April 11, 2020. https://www.holocaustremembranceproject.com/Countries/Slovakia.

Hourani, Albert. *A History of the Arab Peoples*. London: Faber & Faber, 2002.

Human Rights Monitoring Institute. "Hate Speech in Lithuania." Accessed April 10, 2020. https://hrmi.lt/wp-content/uploads/2016/08/Neapykantos_kurstymas_EN.pdf.

Human Rights Watch. *Discrimination in the Name of Neutrality: Headscarf Bans for Teachers and Civil Servants in Germany*. New York: HRW, 2009.

________. *World Report 2020*. Washington DC: HRW, 2020.

Hvidt, Nanna, and Hans Mouritzen, eds. *Danish Foreign Policy Yearbook 2007*. Copenhagen, Danish Institute for International Studies, 2007.

Index on Censorship. "Free Speech Fundamentalist On a Martyrdom Operation." November 11, 2004. Accessed April 5, 2020. https://web.archive.org/web/20041122074958/http://www.indexonline.org/news/vangogh.shtml.

Institut national de la statistique et des études économiques. "2016 Demographic Review." January 17, 2017. Accessed April 1, 2020. https://www.insee.fr/fr/statistiques/2554860.

International, Amnesty. *Report 2013 the State of the World's Human Rights*. London: Amnesty International, 2013.

________. *Report 2017/18: The State of the World's Human Rights.* London: Amnesty International, 2018.

Islamic Parliament of Iran. "The Constitution of the Islamic Republic of Iran." Accessed February 27, 2021. https://en.parliran.ir/eng/en/Constitution.

Istanbul Process. "Istanbul Process." Accessed April 4, 2021. https://www.istanbulprocess1618.info/16-18-process/.

Jackson, Patrick. "Paris Attacks: 'I Am Not Charlie'.: BBC News. January 13, 2015. Accessed April 4, 2021. https://www.bbc.com/news/world-europe-30790412.

Jensen, Sidsel Vive, and Lene Kühle. "School Islam: Lived Religion in the Context of a Secular Public Institution." In *Everyday Lived Islam in Europe*. New York: Routledge, 2013.

John, Tara. "What to Know About Geert Wilders, the 'Dutch Trump'." *Time*, March 10, 2017.

Jones, Nicky. "Beneath the Veil: Muslim Girls and Islamic Headscarves in Secular France." *Macquarie Law Journal* 9 (2009): 47–52.

Kettani, Houssain. "Muslim Population in Europe: 1950–2020." *International Journal of Environmental Science and Development* 1, no. 2 (2010): 155.

Klausen, Jytte. *The Cartoons That Shook the World.* New Haven, CT: Yale University Press, 2009.

Larsson, Göran, ed. *Islam in the Nordic and Baltic Countries.* London: Routledge, 2009.

Law Spot. "Law 927/1979 - Public Endorsement or Denial of Crimes." Accessed April 10, 2020. https://www.lawspot.gr/nomikes-plirofories/nomothesia/n-927-1979/arthro-2-nomos-927-1979-dimosia-epidokimasia-i-arnisi.

Laws of Bangladesh. "The Constitution of the People's Republic of Bangladesh." Accessed February 27, 2021. http://bdlaws.minlaw.gov.bd/act-367/section-24549.html.

Legal Data and Information Network System. "The 1945 Constitution of the Republic of Indonesia." Accessed March 6, 2021. https://jdih.bapeten.go.id/unggah/dokumen/peraturan/116-full.pdf.

Legifrance. "Law of 9 december 1905 concerning the separation of churches and the state." Accessed April 18, 2020. https://www.legifrance.gouv.fr/affichTexte.do?cidTexte=LEGITEXT000006070169&dateTexte=20160802.

Library of Congress. "Limits On Freedom of Expression: France." Accessed April 4, 2020. https://www.loc.gov/law/help/freedom-expression/france.php#_ftnref16.

Lovdata. "The Constitution of the Kingdom of Norway." Accessed April 13, 2020. https://lovdata.no/dokument/NLE/lov/1814-05-17?q=grunnloven.

MENA Rights. "Law No (3) for the Year 2006 On Press and Publications (Kuwait)." Accessed March 10, 2021. https://menarights.org/sites/default/files/2019-01/KWT_PressAndPublicationsLaw_EN.pdf.

________. "The Penal Code for the Year 1960 (Jordan)." Accessed March 8, 2021. https://menarights.org/sites/default/files/2016-11/JOR_PenalCode2011_ENG.pdf.

Margolis, Hillary. "Denmark's Face Veil Ban Latest in Harmful Trend." Human Rights Watch. June 1, 2018. Accessed April 25, 2020. https://www.hrw.org/news/2018/06/01/denmarks-face-veil-ban-latest-harmful-trend.

Marmaduke Pickthall, Mohammed, trans. *The Meaning of the Glorious Quran*. New York: Alfred A. Knopf, 1930.

Marranci, Gabriele. "Multiculturalism, Islam and the Clash of Civilizations Theory: Rethinking Islamophobia." *Culture and Religion: An Interdisciplinary Journal* 5, no. 1 (2004): 105–17.

McGraw, Peter, and Joel Warner. *The Humor Code: A Global Search for What Makes Things Funny.* New York: Simon and Shuster, 2014.

Mela. "Emergency Ordinance no. 31/2002." Accessed April 11, 2020. http://melaproject.org/node/226.

Migration Policy Institute. "Restrictions On Islamic Dress in Europe." June 2018. Accessed April 8, 2020. https://www.migrationpolicy.org/programs/data-hub/charts/restrictions-islamic-dress-europe.

Mill, John Stuart. *On Liberty*. Boston: Ticknor and Fields, 1863.

Ministry of Foreign Affairs, Islamic Republic of Afghanistan. "The Constitution of Afghanistan." Accessed February 27, 2021. https://www.mfa.gov.af/constitution/chapter-one-state.html.

Ministry of Justice. "The Criminal Code." Accessed April 13, 2020. https://www.legislationline.org/download/id/6443/file/Spain_CC_am2013_en.pdf.

Ministry of Justice and Legal Affairs. "Royal Decree no. 101/96 Promulgating the Basic Statute of the State (Oman)." Accessed March 10, 2021. https://mjla.gov.om/eng/basicstatute.aspx.

Ministry of Justice and Public Security. "The Constitution of the Kingdom of Norway." Accessed April 18, 2020. https://lovdata.no/dokument/NLE/lov/1814-05-17?q=grunnloven.

Muhsin Khan, Muhammad, trans. *Sahih Al-bukhari*. Vol. 8. Riyadh: Darussalam, 1997.

Naamat, Talia, Nina Osin, and Dina Porat, eds. *Legislating for Equality: A Multinational Collection of Non-Discrimination Norms*. Leiden: Martinus Nijhoff, 2012.

National Assembly of Pakistan. "The Constitution of the Islamic Republic of Pakistan." Accessed February 27, 2021. http://www.na.gov.pk/uploads/documents/1549886415_632.pdf.

OHCHR. "Human Rights Documents." Accessed April 3, 2021. https://ap.ohchr.org/documents/alldocs.aspx.

OIC. "Islamophobia." Accessed April 4, 2021. https://www.oic-oci.org/page/?p_id=182&p_ref=61&lan=en.

OSCE. "Joint Declaration On Defamation of Religions, and Anti-Terrorism and Anti-Extremism Legislation." December 9, 2008. Accessed April 11, 2020. https://www.osce.org/fom/35639?download=true.

Office for National Statistics. "Population Estimates." Accessed April 1, 2020. https://www.ons.gov.uk/peoplepopulationandcommunity/populationandmigration/populationestimates.

Official Gazette of the Republic of Italy. "Law of June 16, 2016." July 13, 2016. Accessed April 10, 2020. https://www.gazzettaufficiale.it/eli/id/2016/06/28/16G00124/sg.

O'Brien, Peter. *The Muslim Question in Europe: Political Controversies and Public Philosophies*. Philadelphia: Temple University Press, 2016.

Parliament of Germany. "Basic Law for the Federal Republic of Germany." Accessed April 18, 2020. https://www.btg-bestellservice.de/pdf/80201000.pdf.

Parliament of Sweden. "The Constitution of Sweden." Accessed April 18, 2020. https://www.riksdagen.se/globalassets/07.-dokument--lagar/the-constitution-of-sweden-160628.pdf.

Parliament of UK. "Article 9 of the Bill of Rights 1689: An Act Declaring the Rights and Liberties of the Subject, and Settling the Succession of the Crown." Accessed April 3, 2020. https://publications.parliament.uk/pa/jt199899/jtselect/jtpriv/43/4306.htm.

________. "Article 9 of the Bill of Rights 1689: An Act Declaring the Rights and Liberties of the Subject, and Settling the Succession of the Crown." Accessed April 4, 2020. https://publications.parliament.uk/pa/jt199899/jtselect/jtpriv/43/4306.htm.

Perfetti, Alessandro. "Genocide Denial and Freedom of Expression." Master's thesis, LUISS Guido Carli, 2015/2016. Accessed April 10, 2020. https://tesi.luiss.it/id/eprint/16915.

Petersen, Jesper. *The Making of a Mosque with Female Imams: Serendipities in the Production of Danish Islams.* Leiden: Kolninklijke Brill, 2022.

Pew Forum. "Europe's Growing Muslim Population." November 29, 2017. Accessed April 1, 2020. http://www.pewforum.org/2017/11/29/europes-growing-muslim-population/.

________. "The Future of the Global Muslim Population Projections for 2010-2030." January 27, 2011. Accessed April 1, 2020. https://www.pewforum.org/2011/01/27/the-future-of-the-global-muslim-population/.

________. "Religious Composition by Country, 2010-2050." April 02, 2015. Accessed April 1, 2020. http://www.pewforum.org/2015/04/02/religious-projection-table/2010/percent/all/.

Pitkin, Hanna Fenichel. "Are Freedom and Liberty Twins?" *Political Theory* 16, no. 4 (November 1988): 523–52.

Polakow-Suransky, Sasha. *Go Back to Where You Came from*. London: C. Hurst and Company, 2017.

President of the Republic. "The Constitution of the Italian Republic." Accessed April 12, 2020. https://www.quirinale.it/allegati_statici/costituzione/costituzione_inglese.pdf.

Quraishy, Bashy, and Jean o'Connor. *ENAR Shadow Report 2004 Denmark*, European Network Against Racism, 2004.

Raaflaub, Kurt, Josiah Ober, and Robert Wallace. *Origins of Democracy in Ancient Greece*. Berkeley: University of California Press, 2007.

Ramberg, Ingrid. "Islamophobia and Its Consequences On Young People." Published as seminar report by European Youth Centre, Budapest, June 6, 2004. Accessed

April 2, 2020. https://book.coe.int/eur/en/youth-other-publications/3203-islamophobia-and-its-consequences-on-young-people.html.

Refworld. "Penal Code (Malaysia) Act no. 574 of 1997." August 7, 1997. Accessed March 6, 2021. https://www.refworld.org/docid/3ae6b5cf0.html.

Richardson, John E. *(Mis)representing Islam: The Racism and Rhetoric of British Broadsheet Newspapers.* Amsterdam: John Benjamins Publishing Company, 2004.

Riis, Ole. "Religious Pluralism in a Local and Global Perspective: Images of the Prophet Muhammad Seen in a Danish and a Global Context." In *Religion, Globalization, and Culture*, 435. Leiden: Brill, 2007.

Rosentiel, Tom. "The French-Muslim Connection." Pew Research. August 17, 2006. Accessed March 26, 2021. https://www.pewresearch.org/2006/08/17/the-french-muslim-connection/.

Roy, Olivier. "The Nature of the French Riots." SSRC. November 18, 2005. Accessed March 26, 2021. https://items.ssrc.org/riots-in-france/the-nature-of-the-french-riots/.

Rytter, Mikkel. *Family Upheaval: Generation, Mobility, and Relatedness Among Pakistani Migrants in Denmark.* New York: Berghahn Books, 2013.

Senate of the Republic. "Constitution of the Italian Republic." Accessed April 18, 2020. https://www.senato.it/documenti/repository/istituzione/costituzione_inglese.pdf.

Statistics Denmark. "Denmark in Figures 2018." Accessed April 1, 2020. https://www.dst.dk/en/Statistik/Publikationer/VisPub?cid=28923.

Statistisches Bundesamt. "Population by Sex and Citizenship." Accessed April 1, 2020. https://www.destatis.de/EN/FactsFigures/SocietyState/Population/CurrentPopulation/Tables/Census_SexAndCitizenship.html.

Syrian e-Gov Web Portal. "Constitution of the Syrian Arab Republic Approved in Popular Referendum On February 24, 2012." February 24, 2012. Accessed March 29, 2021. https://egov.sy/page/en/137/0/Constitution.html.

The (Saudi) Shura Council. "The Basic Law of Government." March 2, 1992. Accessed March 7, 2021. https://www.shura.gov.sa/wps/wcm/connect/ShuraEn/internet/Laws+and+Regulations/The+Basic+Law+Of+Government.

The Berkley Center for Religion, Peace, and World Affairs. "National Laws On Blasphemy: Spain." Accessed April 15, 2020. https://berkleycenter.georgetown.edu/essays/national-laws-on-blasphemy-spain.

The Church of England. "Leadership and Governance." Accessed April 18, 2020. https://www.churchofengland.org/about/leadership-and-governance.

The Danish Parliament. "The Constitution of the Danish Kingdom." Accessed April 12, 2020. https://www.ft.dk/da/dokumenter/bestil-publikationer/publikationer/grundloven/danmarks-riges-grundlov/kapitel-3/paragraf-13.

________. "The Constitutiona l Act of Denmark." June 5, 1953. Accessed April 10, 2020. https://www.thedanishparliament.dk/-/media/pdf/publikationer/english/the_constitutional_act_of_denmark_2013,-d-,pdf.ashx.

The Federal Council. "Federal Constitution of the Swiss Confederation." April 18, 1999. Accessed April 10, 2020. https://www.admin.ch/opc/en/classified-compilation/19995395/index.html.

________. "Swiss Criminal Code." March 3, 2020. Accessed April 11, 2020. https://www.admin.ch/opc/de/classified-compilation/19370083/index.html#a261bis.

The Federal Government. "Basic Law for the Federal Republic of Germany." Accessed April 8, 2020. https://www.bundesregierung.de/breg-en/chancellor/basic-law-470510.

The Federal Ministry for European and International Affairs. "Islam Law 2015." Accessed April 16, 2020. https://www.bmeia.gv.at/fileadmin/user_upload/Zentrale/Integration/Islamgesetz/Islam_Law_-_Summary.pdf.

The Judicial System. "The Constitution of the Kingdom of the Netherlands 2002." Accessed April 18, 2020. https://www.rechtspraak.nl/SiteCollectionDocuments/Constitution-NL.pdf.

The Legal Information System of the Republic of Austria. "Criminal." Accessed April 13, 2020. https://www.ris.bka.gv.at/Dokument.wxe?Abfrage=Bundesnormen&Dokumentnummer=NOR12029737.

The National Assembly of the State of Kuwait. "The Kuwaiti Constitution." Accessed March 9, 2021. http://www.kna.kw/clt-html5/run.asp?id=2024.

The Riksdag. "The Constitution of Sweden." Accessed April 13, 2020. https://www.riksdagen.se/globalassets/07.-dokument--lagar/the-constitution-of-sweden-160628.pdf.

The Swiss Confederation. "Swiss Criminal Code." Accessed April 15, 2020. https://www.admin.ch/opc/en/classified-compilation/19370083/202003030000/311.0.pdf.

The White House. "Remarks by the President Upon Arrival, the South Lawn." September 16, 2001. Accessed April 1, 2020. http://georgewbush-whitehouse.archives.gov/news/releases/2001/09/20010916-2.html.

The Federal Legal Information System (RIS). "Anti-Facial Covering Law." Accessed April 17, 2020. https://www.ris.bka.gv.at/GeltendeFassung.wxe?Abfrage=Bundesnormen&Gesetzesnummer=20009892.

UK Legislation. "Human Rights Act 1998." Accessed April 18, 2020. http://www.legislation.gov.uk/ukpga/1998/42/section/13.

________. "Crown Proceedings Act 1947." Accessed April 13, 2020. http://www.legislation.gov.uk/ukpga/Geo6/10-11/44/contents.

UN General Assembly. "Resolution Adopted by the Human Rights Council." March 25, 2010. Accessed April 9, 2020. https://undocs.org/A/HRC/RES/13/16.

UN Human Rights. "France: Banning the Niqab Violated Two Muslim Women's Freedom of Religion." October 23, 2018. Accessed April 7, 2020. https://www.ohchr.org/EN/NewsEvents/Pages/DisplayNews.aspx?NewsID=23750&LangID=E.

________. "International Covenant On Economic, Social and Cultural Rights." December 16, 1966. Accessed April 9, 2020. https://www.ohchr.org/en/professionalinterest/pages/cescr.aspx.

UNESCO. "Constitution of the Republic of Iceland." Accessed April 12, 2020. http://www.unesco.org/education/edurights/media/docs/2d641c3d0298f84279ec1b3bc6e313a0a3770987.pdf.

UNGA. "57/208. Elimination of All Forms of Religious Intolerance." February 14, 2003. Accessed April 3, 2021. https://undocs.org/en/A/RES/57/208.

US Department of State. “Austria 2018 International Religious Freedom Report.” Accessed April 19, 2020. https://www.state.gov/wp-content/uploads/2019/05/AUSTRIA-2018-INTERNATIONAL-RELIGIOUS-FREEDOM-REPORT.pdf.

United Nations. “Dialogue Among Civilizations: Contexts and Perspectives.” Accessed April 4, 2021. https://www.un.org/en/chronicle/article/dialogue-among-civilizations-contexts-and-perspectives.

________. “General Assembly Resolutions.” Accessed April 3, 2021. https://www.un.org/en/sections/documents/general-assembly-resolutions/index.html.

________. “International Convention On the Elimination of All Forms of Racial Discrimination.” January 4, 1969. Accessed April 4, 2020. https://treaties.un.org/Pages/ViewDetails.aspx?src=TREATY&mtdsg_no=IV-2&chapter=4&clang=_en.

________. “International Covenant On Civil and Political Rights.” Accessed April 3, 2020. https://treaties.un.org/doc/publication/unts/volume%20999/volume-999-i-14668-english.pdf.

________. “Universal Declaration of Human Rights.” Accessed April 3, 2020. https://www.un.org/en/udhrbook/pdf/udhr_booklet_en_web.pdf.

United Nations Office on Drugs and Crime. “Polish Penal Code.” Accessed April 14, 2020. https://www.unodc.org/res/cld/document/pol/1997/penal_code_html/Poland_Penal_Code_1997.pdf.

WIPO. “Syrian Penal Code (Arabic).” Accessed March 29, 2021. https://www.wipo.int/edocs/lexdocs/laws/ar/sy/sy013ar.pdf.

Weller, Paul. *A Mirror for Our Times: ‘the Rushdie affair’ and the Future of Multiculturalism*. London: Bloomsbury Academic, 2009.

Whine, Michael. “Expanding Holocaust Denial and Legislation Against It.” *Jewish Political Studies Review* 20, no. 1 (Spring 2008): 62.

World Population Review. “Muslim Majority Countries 2021.” Accessed March 23, 2021. https://worldpopulationreview.com/country-rankings/muslim-majority-countries.

Index

About the Author

Haris bin Aziz is currently a postdoctoral visiting fellow at the Department of International History, London School of Economics and Political Science. He earned his PhD in European studies from Area Study Centre for Europe, University of Karachi and remained visiting doctoral scholar at the University of Cambridge, Columbia University, King's College London, and the University of Bologna. Haris has held visiting academic positions at SOAS, Queen Mary University of London, and Goldsmiths University of London. Working as a journalist with renowned Pakistani organizations since 2005, Haris has remained fellow of the Center for Media, Data and Society, Central European University; Knight-Salzburg Fellow in 2009; FES Af-Pak Journalism Fellow in 2012; and Dora Plus Visiting Doctoral Scholar at the Tallinn University of Technology in 2018. He has taught European studies to MPhil students and international relations to graduate students at the University of Karachi and conducted research at the Pakistan Institute of International Affairs and Social Policy and Development Center, Karachi.

www.ingramcontent.com/pod-product-compliance
Ingram Content Group UK Ltd.
Pitfield, Milton Keynes, MK11 3LW, UK
UKHW041839031026
15587UKWH00002B/882

9 781666 934700